girl in the curl

A CENTURY OF WOMEN IN SURFING

Andrea Gabbard

Seal Press

In memory of the spirit of Rell Sunn
and in honor of the grace of Marge Calhoun

Front cover design by Tom Adler
Front cover photograph by Tom Servais
Back cover photograph by Jim Russi
Interior design and layout by Alison Rogalsky

All interior photographs without captions are copyright © Jim Russi.

"The Women of Malibu," by Jeff Duclos, originally appeared in *Longboard*, May/June 1999.
Reprinted by permission of the author.

Library of Congress Cataloging-in-Publication Data
Gabbard, Andrea.
Girl in the curl : a century of women in surfing / Andrea Gabbard.
p. cm.
Includes bibliographical references.
ISBN 1-58005-048-4 (paper)
1. Surfing for women. 2. Surfers—Biography. I. Title.

GV840.S8 G22 2000
797.3'2'082—dc21   00-057388

Printed in Hong Kong by Midas Printing
First printing, December 2000

10   9   8   7   6   5   4   3   2   1

Distributed to the trade by Publishers Group West
In Canada: Publishers Group West Canada, Toronto, Ontario
In Australia: Banyan Tree Book Distributors, Kent Town, South Australia

Opposite: Megan Abubo
Photo: Jim Russi

CONTENTS

ACKNOWLEDGMENTS

The biggest challenge in writing this book was selecting the women to profile. Many people helped develop my list. For their suggestions and guidance, I am grateful. I understood from the outset that it would be impossible to include every woman who ever surfed. I knew women worthy of mention wouldn't make it into these pages or would end up only briefly mentioned. To these women, I apologize. The women profiled here either contributed to the advancement of surfing, inspired other women or helped them gain proficiency. Above all, they were accessible and willing to share their stories.

This book would not have been possible without the generosity of Randy Hild, vice president of Roxy/Quiksilver, who helped propel this project along from the beginning and made his extensive archives available. Tom Adler applied his expert art direction. Allan Seymour served as an inimitable behind-the-scenes advisor. Karin Moeller contributed several excellent stories, photographs and research for the glossary and resources.

Mary Hartman graciously encouraged my use of the title *Girl in the Curl*, which happens to be the name of the women's surf shop she founded in 1997 in Dana Point, California. When Mary's not in the shop or at school, she's "in the curl."

My sister-in-law, Deneece, who is producing a documentary on women in surfing, accompanied me on most interviews, including an extensive fact-finding trip to Hawaii in December 1999. Our other sis-in-law, Arlene, traveled with us to assist with camera and recording equipment, and kept us upbeat with her easygoing spirit. Girls, I look forward to our next project!

I wish to thank others who graciously donated time and assistance, including Malia Alani and Melissa Calvano of *Surfer*, Elizabeth Glazner of *Wahine*, Steve Pezman of *Surfer's Journal,* Jessica Trent and Michael Marckx. I am grateful to the photographers whose beautiful images grace this book. A heartfelt thank you to Jim Russi for his exceptional photographs and generosity, along with Leroy Grannis, Tom Servais, Jeff Divine, Bernie Baker, John Severson, Art Brewer and Jeff Hornbaker. And, a special nod to Tomas Gibson, Elizabeth Pepin, Heidi and Ray Vetter, Joe and Aggie Quigg. Thanks also to Glen and Meredith Moncata, Momi Keaulana, Kathy Terada, Fred Hemmings, Randy Rarick, Ken Bradshaw, Renato Hickel, Jack Shipley, Robin Janiszeufski, Laurie Houk, Danielle Beck, Amy Patrick, Mike Doyle, Midget Smith, Jeff Duclos, Lance Carson and, of course, the interviewees.

Faith Conlon, my publisher, spent a weekend at San Onofre in October 1999 at the Roxy Wahine Classic surf contest and got stoked on the project immediately. Thanks to Faith and Seal Press staff for helping me stay on track and on time. The creative talents of Lee Damsky and Alison Rogalsky in producing the book are inestimable.

My fellow editors at *Outdoor Retailer* shared the surf and gave support and feedback. Numerous other associates shared enthusiasm and information; special appreciation goes to Stacey White, Linda Bowers and Water Girl apparel company's Alison Cutler.

My family and friends provide a solid foundation of love and support for which I am grateful. Francey cheerfully relieves everyday burdens and always lends a patient ear. Lacey, Sam, Walt, Jacki, Jessi and Justin inspire me to think young. At zero hour deadline, Pam buoyed my spirits when she stated, "The anchor's always heavier just before it comes up."

My mother, who now exists in spirit, introduced my brothers and me to the water before we could walk, instilling in us a lifelong love of the ocean and water sports. I am forever grateful. She would have liked this book.

TIMELINE

?–1700s: Polynesians and Hawaiians enjoy surfing as part of their culture.

Late 1700s: Infectious diseases spread by Captain Cook's men nearly decimates native Hawaiian population.

1800s: Puritanical missionaries declare surfing a heathen pastime; sport nearly dies out.

1900: Visiting businessmen and journalists witness Duke Kahanamoku, brothers and friends surfing Waikiki; sport begins to enjoy resurrection.

1907: Hawaiian George Freeth introduces surfing to Southern California.

1912: Kahanamoku wins Olympic Gold Medal in swimming; becomes Hawaii's unofficial swimming and surfing ambassador.

1915: Kahanamoku introduces surfing to Australia; teaches 15-year-old Isobel Letham to surf.

1920s: Hawaii becomes popular cruise and vacation destination; Waikiki beach boys teach tourists to surf and paddle outrigger canoes.

1931: Pete Peterson and Lorrin Harrison discover tandem surfing in Hawaii and bring it home to California.

1930s and 1940s: Ethel Harrison learns to surf in California, moves to Hawaii and marries Hawaiian surfer Joe Kukea; Mary Ann (Hawkins) Morrissey rides her redwood board at Pacific Palisades and San Onofre.

1940s and 1950s: Servicemen and women stationed in Hawaii discover surfing; Keanuinui Rochlen distinguishes herself as one of Hawaii's finest paddlers and surfers; Makaha and Waikiki become prime surfing areas.

Late 1940s, early 1950s: Malibu, California becomes a popular surfing spot; Robin Grigg, Aggie Bane, Vicki Flaxman, Claire Cassidy, Darilyn Zanuck Zinc, Marge Gleason, Patty O'Keefe, Barbara Peterson and Diane Griffith make up the distaff side of the surfing community.

1950: Joe Quigg introduces a shorter, lighter, maneuverable balsawood "Girl Board" to the women of Malibu who, in turn, change the way waves are ridden.

1952: Makaha International Surfing Championship founded by Wally Froiseth and Waikiki Surf Club.

1954: Ethel Kukea wins women's division of Makaha International Surfing Championship (repeats the win in 1955); Walter Hoffman and Joan Jones win first tandem division trophy in 1954.

Mid-1950s: The waves of Oahu's North Shore are finally ridden and the area quickly becomes surfing's Mecca; Marge Calhoun learns to surf at Malibu.

1956: Gidget goes to Malibu; her father's book, *Gidget,* is published in 1957.

1958: Marge Calhoun wins Makaha International Surfing Championship at age thirty-something; surfs the North Shore with Eve Fletcher.

1959: The first U.S. Championships is held in Huntington Beach and is won by 15-year-old Linda Benson, who also wins Makaha International Surfing Championship; the movie, *Gidget,* is released; Linda Merrill wins her first contest.

Early 1960s: A wave of beach party movies provides stunt work for many surfers and also attracts inland America to the beach.

1960: Joyce Hoffman starts surfing, wins the Makaha International in 1964 and five world titles between 1966 and 1971.

1963: Linda Merrill and Mike Doyle win the Makaha International tandem event; Shelley Merrick wins her first contest at Dockweiler Beach at age seventeen.

1964: Australian Phyllis O'Donnell captures first world amateur championship.

1965: Mimi Munro wins East Coast Championship at age thirteen in Wrightsville Beach, North Carolina; she repeats her wins in 1966 and 1967.

1966: Barrie (Algaw) Boehne and Pete Peterson win fourteen tandem events in a row, including the U.S. Championships, the Makaha International and the World Contest in San Diego; Margo (Godfrey) Oberg is ranked fourth in the world at age thirteen.

1967 to present: Barrie and Steve Boehne become tandem partners and take the sport to a new level; they also marry and open a surf shop.

1968: Margo (Godfrey) Oberg wins her first of numerous world titles at age fifteen, marking the start of a pro career that spans three decades; the shortboard is introduced and changes the face of surfing.

1972: Mary Setterholm wins U.S. Championships in Huntington Beach.

1974: Rell Sunn starts annual Menehune Contest at Makaha.

1975: Women's International Surfing Association (WISA) formed by Mary Setterholm, Jericho Poppler and Mary Lou (McGinnis) Drummy; first WISA contest held at Malibu; Wendy Gilley turns pro.

1976: International Professional Surfing (IPS), an organization formed by Fred Hemmings, incorporates a women's tour.

1977: Margo Oberg opens her surfing school on Kauai.

1978: Lynn Boyer wins first of two consecutive world titles.

1979: Women's Pro Surfing (WPS) formed by pro women Jericho Poppler, Rell Sunn, Lynne Boyer, Margo Oberg, Cherie Gross, Linda Davoli, Debbie Beacham, Becky Benson and Brenda Scott.

1982: Seventeen-year-old Floridian Frieda Zamba wins the Mazda Surfsports Pro in Solana Beach, California, and begins her ten-year dominance over women's surfing; Pam Burridge turns pro at age sixteen and becomes Australia's first professional surfer; Debbie Beacham wins world title.

1983: Kim Mearig wins world title; newly formed Association of Surfing Professionals (ASP) takes over men and women's pro circuit; Debbie Beacham serves on the ASP board until 1991.

1984: Frieda Zamba wins the first of four world titles; Australian Jodie Cooper turns pro; Surfrider Foundation founded to preserve the ocean environment.

1986: Lisa Andersen turns pro at age seventeen.

1987: Wendy Botha wins the first of four world titles.

1990: Pam Burridge wins world title; Rochelle Ballard turns pro.

1991: Last WISA-sponsored contest held.

1992: Margo Oberg surfs her last pro contest; Jericho Poppler starts Jericho's Kids for Clean Waves contest and outreach program.

1993: Pauline Menczer wins world title.

1994: Lisa Andersen wins the first of four consecutive world titles.

1995: Water Girl, first all-woman's surf shop, opened in Encinitas, California; *Wahine*, first all-women's surf magazine, launched.

1996: Lisa Andersen is featured on the cover of *Surfer* with the caption, "Lisa Andersen surfs better than you"; Isabelle "Izzy" Tihanyi opens Surf Diva, first all-women's surf school in La Jolla, California.

1997: East Coast Wahine Championships debuts in Wrightsville Beach, North Carolina; Las Olas surf camp for women founded near Puerto Vallarta by Bev Sanders.

1998: In January, Rell Sunn, beloved "Queen of Makaha," succumbs to cancer; Layne Beachley wins the first of two consecutive world titles.

1999: Australian Trudy Todd wins the women's Triple Crown title in Hawaii.

2000: Women's surfing enters a new era.

girl in the curl

Lisa Andersen, Rochelle Ballard and Roxy
Team Manager Danielle Beck on their way to
practice, Sunset Beach, Hawaii.
Photo: Andrea Gabbard

Introduction

During the summer of 1960, just before my thirteenth birthday, I learned to surf at Doheny Beach in Southern California with my two closest girlfriends, Natalia and Jennifer. Natalia's dad enjoyed scuba diving at Doheny with a buddy who had an old, heavy, eleven-foot-plus surfboard that we could play around on.

Natalia, Jennifer and I were beach rats. We grew up with our brothers body surfing and riding waves on rubber beach mats. The progression to a hard surfboard was only daunting in that it took all three of us to carry it down to the water. Once waterborne, the board glided along smoothly and was easy to stand up on. We quickly badgered our folks into buying us "real" surfboards. My first board was ten feet long and weighed nearly forty pounds.

by Andrea Gabbard

Until our senior year, we were the only surfer girls in our high school. Plenty of guys had taken up the sport. We'd see each other along the coast at our favorite spots, from Huntington Beach to San Diego. During school vacations, Jennifer's dad drove us to Baja to surf. As soon as we got licenses, we drove ourselves. We surfed year-round on weekends and every day that we could during summer break. We listened to Dick Dale, the Beach Boys and other surf bands—proud to be part of the world's only sport with its own music.

None of us owned a wetsuit. In winter, as soon as we were about fifteen minutes from the beach, we'd turn off the car's heater, roll down the windows and have a "freeze out" to get acclimated to the cold. We knew it was time to come in from the water when Jennifer's lips turned blue.

Surfing was carefree and friendly until the mid-to-late sixties, when the waves began to seem crowded to those of us who had grown up with plenty of waves for all. Suddenly, we didn't recognize everyone in the water. And, sometimes, we got hassled by guys who would cut us off on waves. At the same time, college and careers were beckoning, and Natalia, Jennifer and I drifted away from the sport. But our friendship remained intact.

More than thirty years later, while researching this book, I found myself at La Jolla Cove in California with a trio of instructors from Surf Diva, an all-women's surf school founded by surfer Isabelle

Surfing buddies Jennifer Mitchell, Natalia Rez, Andrea Gabbard, Larry Brown and Clifford Mitchell. Doheny Beach, 1962.
Photo: Natalia Corich

"Izzy" Tihanyi. The two-to-four-foot surf looked big enough to me. With Izzy's encouragement, I stood up and rode a wave on my third try. That ride was nearly as satisfying as the first time I stood up at Doheny. My early surfing career lasted only six years, but the feeling of surfing never left me, probably because it is so strongly tied to my love of the ocean. Yet surfing is not like riding a bike. I discovered that I couldn't just jump back on and go—at least not at the level of my teens. Even so, I am committed to enjoying the sport again, especially after this memorable encounter: I caught a small wave and rode it to shore, where I hopped off and turned around immediately to paddle back out. Two young men passed me in the water. One smiled and said, "Next time, we want to see you hang ten." Guys are getting used to seeing women in the waves.

In Hawaii, conducting more research, I ran into Australian pro surfer Matt Hoy. I asked him how he felt about more women taking up the sport. He responded, typically, "It's great, I like women in and out of the water." On a more serious note, he added, "It's nice to mix it up. All blokes all the time gets a little boring." A couple of months later at Malibu, the legendary Lance Carson (who was participating in a Surfrider Foundation beach cleanup) offered this insight: "I don't know why we didn't want women in the water in the old days. It was okay if they hung out on the beach with us, but they weren't supposed to surf. It was just one of those macho things. Today, I think it's great. Most of the women out surfing are better than half the guys."

Perhaps this is true because it is easier than ever to learn to surf. Surfboards are lighter (averaging seven to fifteen pounds) and easier to carry and maneuver. Leashes prevent surfboards from drifting to shore and necessitating a long swim. (Many surfers from the fifties and sixties have a different view of this supposed advancement, noting that leashes, while beneficial, have fostered weaker swimmers and paddlers among both men and women. Surfers from this era often worked as lifeguards and participated in paddling contests; they prided themselves on their swimming and paddling prowess.) There are more surf camps, surf schools and surf clinics than ever before, many of which cater only to women. Also, the gear is reasonable: The average cost of a new surfboard is around five hundred dollars. According to veteran shaper Steve Boehne, owner of Infinity Surf in Dana Point, California, the price of a surfboard has only increased five-fold since 1960, while cars have gone up sixteen times and homes twenty-two.

There also are more places to surf, thanks to surfers who have traveled the world in search of waves. Today, surf spots exist on nearly every coastline of every continent, and on islands around the world, particularly in Tahiti and Indonesia. France, Spain, Japan, Brazil and South Africa have joined California, Hawaii, Peru and Australia as competition host sites. And Florida is now producing champion surfers!

Early postcard from Hawaii, circa 1920s. Roxy collection

For women—and men—interested in competition, there are several amateur programs as well as a professional tour. Amateur contests provide an enjoyable way to meet other surfers, sharpen skills and gain competitive experience. Today's pros compete in a regular circuit of events around the globe, but this was not always so.

From the fifties through the early seventies, single invitational contests in places such as Hawaii, Peru and Australia were considered the deciding events for the surfing world champion. Most of these contests included a women's division. The key word here is "invitational." As one former pro surfer stated, "If you didn't get invited to compete, it didn't matter how good you were, you sure weren't going to be champion that year!" Contest organizers relied both on first-hand knowledge and word-of-mouth recommendations to bring together a competitive field that usually included the current cream of the crop.

In 1976, world champion surfer Fred Hemmings formed International Professional Surfing (IPS), an organization that coordinated the first international circuit of professional events, with an accumulating point system to determine the champion each year. In 1982, the Association of Surfing Professionals (ASP) overthrew Hemmings' circuit and established its own, complete with sponsors. The ASP was composed of a group of surfers led by former pro Ian Cairns. Represented by their own association, Women's Pro Surfing (WPS), women agreed at that time to come in under the ASP umbrella and have been there ever since.

Today, the ASP maintains two competitive rosters each for men and women: The World Qualifying Series (WQS) and the World Championship Tour (WCT). The women's WCT is composed of fourteen contenders: The top nine women from the previous year's WCT rankings and the top five from the WQS. A surfer can enter a WQS event simply by paying the seventy-five dollar entry fee. The WQS is designed to be a qualifying tour on which a surfer earns points as well as competition experience against some of the top surfers in the world. The WCT is the road that leads to world champion.

Despite the organization of a pro tour and the advent of financial sponsors, professional women surfers have always suffered a fate similar to that of other female athletes, pursuing their sport with far less promotion, prize money and media coverage. Even the *Gidget* books, movie and television series and the spate of Hollywood beach party films that followed in the sixties did little to relieve women's professional surfing of its backseat position. Joyce Hoffman, who captured several world titles in the sixties, says, "Maybe it's

1966 Makaha International finalists: l to r, Joey Hamasaki, Margo Oberg, Joyce Hoffman, Phyllis O'Donnell, Martha Sunn, Patty Powers. Photo: LeRoy Grannis

better this way. Then women will compete for the love of the sport, rather than for the money."

Current pros do not share Hoffman's sentiment. As surfing enters a new millennium and women's professional sports gain more exposure, media acceptance and sponsorship, women's pro surfing is beginning to stand on its own. The economic base supporting women's pro surfing is far greater now than in the seventies and eighties. The 1990s saw the introduction of many women's surf apparel lines, from new companies as well as the most prominent labels in men's surfwear such as Quiksilver (with Roxy, its junior women's brand), Billabong, Gotcha (with GirlStar), Rusty, Ocean Pacific (Op) and O'Neill. A few pros earn a decent living from surfing. In 1999, World Champion Layne Beachley finished the year with over $65,000 in prize money, plus sponsorship earnings (the 1999 men's champion, Mark Occhilupo, earned $89,700 in prize money). Only a handful of the top women, including Beachley, Lisa Andersen, Serena Brooke and Rochelle Ballard, have lucrative sponsorship contracts that provide travel expenses and pay bonuses for media exposure and contest results. Most pros pay their own expenses out of contest winnings or family support.

Ultimately, beauty, power and soulfulness define surfing, not sponsorship issues or political jockeying on the basis of gender. The challenges involved in organizing amateur and professional circuits and in securing sponsors and media coverage will continue, just as women will continue to seek their place in the waves.

That place has been secured by a long line of pioneering women surfers, beginning in the early twentieth century. Isobel Letham rode her first wave in Australia in 1915. In the thirties and forties, Californian Mary Ann (Hawkins) Morrisey used to astound beachgoers by lugging her eighty-pound redwood-balsa surfboard up and down the cliff at Palos Verdes in winter, all for the joy of riding waves. In the early fifties, the women of Malibu—including Aggie Bane, Vicki Flaxman and Robin Grigg—changed the way surfers rode waves with their lightweight balsa-wood Girl Boards made by Joe Quigg. Marge Calhoun, who learned to surf at Malibu, charged the big waves of the North Shore of Oahu in 1958. A year later, Linda Benson became the first woman to ride Waimea Bay and the youngest, at fifteen, to win at Makaha. In 1964, Hawaii-based Bernie Ross was the only woman surfer featured in Bruce Brown's epic film,

14 Top: E.J. Oshier and Mary Ann Hawkins surfing San Onofre on redwood boards, late 1930s. Photo: Doc Ball, courtesy LeRoy Grannis.

Bottom: 1970s pioneers, l to r, Lynne Boyer, Margo Oberg, Liz Benevidez, Betty Depolito, Jericho Poppler, Debbie Beacham. Photo: Jeff Divine

Endless Summer. In 1968, Joyce Hoffman paddled out to claim the first woman's ride at Pipeline. In 1974, Laura Blears won a slot in the men's Smirnoff Pro, held in epic surf at Waimea Bay. In the late seventies, "Fearless" Phyllis Dameron started riding huge surf at Waimea Bay and Sunset Beach on her bodyboard and held the distinction of having surfed larger waves than any other woman in history—until the winter of 1998, when Aussie pro Layne Beachley got towed into the thirty-foot face of an offshore-reef wave in Hawaii. In March 1999, twenty-five-year-old Northern California surfer Sarah Gerhardt paddled into surfing history when she became the first woman to ride Mavericks, a dangerous, cold-water wave off California's Half Moon Bay that doesn't break until the face tops twenty-five feet.

The future of women's surfing doesn't lie solely in big surf. The future lies in more women being inspired to ride waves of all sizes and types: beach break, mush, knee-high, head-high, overhead, tubes and monstrous, heaving walls that obliterate the sun. Each woman who ventures into the surf will celebrate many firsts: her first wave, first barrel, first nose ride, first wipe out, first overhead, first surf trip, first ding and first perfect turn where surfer, board and wave move as one. Surfing is a unique experience that bonds the surfer to the ancient people of the world, who respected the sea for its bounty and mystery, and rode its waves with passion and joy. Every surfer knows the feeling.

"Fearless" Phyllis Dameron still rides today.
Sunset Beach. Photo: Bernie Baker

Turnoff to Haleiwa, cornerstone of the North Shore of Oahu.
Photo: Jim Russi

The Birthplace of Modern Surfing

The ocean that surges onto Hawaii's shores has defined its culture—and surfing—for centuries. For the early Hawaiians, the ocean provided a source of inspiration, religion, food and recreation. Both the native royalty, called Ali'i, and commoners enjoyed the sport of surfing—although commoners were prohibited from surfing at the same time as the royals—and surfers of both sexes rode the waves together.

Hawaii is uniquely located in the path of groundswells generated by storm centers in both the North and South Pacific. Sandy beaches, coral reefs, lava headlands, lagoons and curving bays all contribute their own type of wave riding condition, from gentle combers to giant crushing monsters.

The most ancient Hawaiian legends tell of Pele, Goddess of Volcanoes, surfing. According to legend, the *aumakua* (guardian) shark god Kamohoali'I taught Pele how to surf; Pele taught her sister Hi'iaka and soon the men got involved. Hundreds of years later, in the 1700s, Captain Cook sailed into Kealakekua Bay, where he and his crew witnessed natives performing feats on wooden planks in the breaking waves. Historians believe that, for at least a couple thousand years, children and adults throughout the Pacific rode waves lying on short, flat pieces of wood—until the Hawaiians reshaped the sport in the 1700s by lengthening the planks and standing up on them.

The early Hawaiians used sizable surfboards, the largest of which were eighteen feet long, two feet wide and several inches thick, weighing 150 pounds or more. Many of these ancient boards are well preserved and are exhibited in Honolulu museums.

For Hawaiian royalty, surfing was especially enticing. Kamehameha I, the king who united the Hawaiian Islands into a single kingdom in the late 1700s and early 1800s, learned to surf along the Kona coast of the island of Hawaii.

Many surf spots on the Islands were sites of romance and ritual among the royalty. A Tahitian chief, Mo'ikeha, sailed in his double-hulled canoe from Tahiti to Kauai, where he joined the natives in surfing the famous curving surf of Makaiwa. From shore, two sisters, who just happened to be the daughters of the ruling chief of Kauai, spied the handsome chief. Mo'ikeha married both of them.

On Oahu, the offshore break known in the 1920s and 1930s as Outside Castles

Pictorial Hawaiian history souvenir postcard. Roxy collection

was originally called Kalehuawehe, "the removed lehua." According to legend, while riding a wave at this spot, a surfer removed his lei made of lehua flower blossoms and presented it to a chiefess who was also surfing there. Another ancient break, called Ke-kai-o-Mamala (the Sea of Mamala), not far from Waikiki and what is now the Honolulu harbor, was named after a famous surfer and prominent Oahu chiefess who was also a *kupua*, or demigod with supernatural powers. She could take the form of a beautiful woman, a lizard or a shark. Mamala became entangled in a love triangle. First married to another *kupua*, the shark-man Ouha, she left him when Honoka'upu, the owner of a beautiful coconut grove, fell in love with her and chose her as his wife. Ouha became so distressed that he cast off his human form, becoming the great shark god of the coast between Oahu and Koko Head.

Sunset Beach, on the North Shore of Oahu, was once called Paumalu. This name means "taken secretly," referring to a woman whose legs were bitten off by a shark after she had taken more octopus than custom permitted. Paumalu always has been known for its huge, thundering waves. Kahikilani, a prince of Kauai, crossed the hundred miles of open ocean between his home and Oahu just to prove himself in the ferocious Paumalu surf. In their book, *Surfing, A History of the Ancient Hawaiian Sport*, authors Ben Finney

HAWAIIAN SPORT OF SURF PLAYING

In the 1700s, both native royalty—Ali'i—and commoners enjoyed the sport of surfing.
Engraving: Bishop Museum

and James D. Houston relate Kahikilani's tale. Anyone who has ever dated a surfer can relate to this story:

> *Day after day, he perfected his skill in the jawlike waves. As he rode he was watched by a bird maiden with supernatural powers who lived in a cave on a nearby mountain. She fell in love with the prince and sent bird messengers to place an orange lehua lei around his neck and bring him to her . . . Enchanted, he spent several months with her—until the return of the surf season. Then the distant sizzle and boom of the waves of Paumalu were too much for Kahikilani to resist, and he left the maiden, but only after promising never to kiss another woman . . . Almost as soon as he was riding again, a beautiful woman came walking along the white sand . . . she placed an ilima lei around his neck and kissed him. His vow was broken. He thought nothing of it and paddled back out to the breaking waves, but the bird messengers were watching . . . When she heard their report, the bird maiden ran to the beach . . . Snatching the ilima lei from Kahikilani's neck, she replaced it with one made with lehua blossoms. As she ran back to her cave, he chased her. That was the last Kahikilani saw of the bird maiden, though, for halfway up the mountain he was turned to stone.*

Finney and Houston's work details early accounts of women surfing:

> *A large percentage of women in ancient Hawaii were skillful surfers, and sometimes champions. A number of early engravings of the sport show island wahine perched on surfboards on top of a curling wave.*
>
> *No doubt many an amorous Hawaiian, who on some days didn't feel at all like surfing, found himself paddling for the breaker line in pursuit of his lady love, knowing full well that if a man and woman happened to ride the same wave together, custom allowed certain intimacies when they returned to the beach. More formal courtship was carried out in the surf, when a man or woman tried to woo and win a mate by performing on the waves. Hawaiian legends abound in tales of thwarted and successful love affairs, and surfing played a part in many of them.*

Top. Outrigger canoeing and surfing postcard from Hawaii. Roxy collection

Bottom: Matson Lines promotional postcard Roxy collection

Kamehameha I and his favorite wife, Ka'ahumanu, were said to be expert surfers. Queen Emma, a member of nineteenth-century Hawaiian royalty, had a surf chant composed in her honor.

In the early 1800s, puritanical New England missionaries arrived in Hawaii and declared surfing a heathen sport. By then, the native population had dwindled from nearly a half million to around forty thousand, decimated by infectious diseases brought ashore by Captain Cook and his men. The once powerful Hawaiian chiefs were unable to muster much resistance to the missionaries' zeal. In his book, *SurfRiders,* Matt Warshaw states: "The missionaries in ten short years convinced the Hawaiians to take up Calvinist-based religion, politics and culture. Surfing wasn't categorically prohibited, but it was boxed out by the new work ethic, along with restrictions on nudity, gaming, and nearly all mixed-sex recreation . . . By 1892, an observer noted, it was 'hard to find a surfboard outside of our museums and private collections.'"

By the turn of the twentieth century, young Hawaiian Duke Kahanamoku, his brothers and friends had started surfing Waikiki. Visiting businessmen saw a potential tourist attraction and journalists took note. Both Mark Twain and Jack London wrote about surfing after visiting "the Islands," as the Hawaiian Islands became known. In the twenties and thirties, Hawaii became a cruise destination and a vacation spot. Surf bathing gained popularity among tourist men *and* women. Hawaiians found gainful employment as "beach boys" at Waikiki hotels, teaching men and women to ride the waves, taking them in outrigger canoes and entertaining them at night with songs and ukulele playing.

Kahanamoku's fame spread beyond Waikiki after he won a gold medal for swimming in the 1912 Olympics in Stockholm. He was thereafter known around the world as Hawaii's ambassador of surfing. In 1915, Kahanamoku accepted an invitation from Australia to give swimming demonstrations. While Down Under, he also performed surfing feats and initiated Australia's first surfer into the sport. That surfer happened to be a young woman, Isobel Letham, who in turn led her countrymen and -women into the waves.

Hawaiian surfer George Freeth is credited with introducing surfing to Southern California in 1907 when he gave surfing demonstrations at Redondo Beach. Heavy wooden Hawaiian surfboards started finding their way to the West Coast and were reproduced by various surfing craftsmen.

In Hawaii, men and women started taking to the surf seriously in the forties and fifties.

A FAIR SURFBOARD RIDER
PHOTO BY BAKER HONOLULU

Top: Duke Kahanamoku surfing Waikiki. Photo: Tom Blake, courtesy Gary Lynch and Roxy collection.

Bottom: "A Fair Surfboard Rider," souvenir postcard. Roxy collection

Servicemen and -women stationed on Oahu wrote home about the beautiful beaches, lovely coconut groves, vast pineapple fields and perfect surf. After World War II, Hawaiian tourism took off, and surfing with it. As the most populous island, Oahu attracted the majority of surfers. Eventually, other surf spots were discovered on Maui, Kauai and the "Big Island" of Hawaii.

Keanuinui Rochlen was heralded as one of the best surfers and outrigger canoe paddlers in the Islands. First married to beach boy Rabbit Kekai, and now to Dave Rochlen, founder of the Surfline apparel company, Keanuinui still competes in long-distance outrigger canoe races. Another woman who influenced women's surfing in Hawaii was Ethel Kukea, the sister of Southern California surfing icon Lorrin "Whitey" Harrison. Ethel learned to surf in the thirties in California, then married into Hawaii's Kukea surfing family.

The Makaha International Surfing Championship on Oahu was launched in 1952 by surf pioneer Wally Froiseth and friends of the Waikiki Surf Club. Unfortunately, due to consistent flat surf conditions the first two winters, the inaugural Makaha contest wasn't held until 1954. A women's division was not scheduled until 1955. Ethel Kukea won that year and the next, and dominated Hawaiian women's surfing for the rest of the decade.

Many women surfers of the fifties, sixties and seventies made their mark in this contest, including Hawaiians Anona (Naone) Napoleon and Martha Sunn and Californians Vicki Heldrich, Marge Calhoun, Linda Benson, Wendy Cameron, Nancy Nelson, Joyce Hoffman, Margo Godfrey Oberg, Becky Benson and Sharon Weber. The contest also included a tandem surfing division. Walt Hoffman—father of world champion Joyce Hoffman—and his tandem partner Joan Jones won the first tandem trophy in 1954.

The North Shore of Oahu wasn't ridden by modern surfers until the mid-fifties. Surfers had been dissuaded by local taboos and the story of a surfer who perished while attempting to paddle from Sunset Beach to Waimea Bay to find safe harbor in dangerous storm surf. After a handful of legendary big wave surfers—including Walt Hoffman, Greg Noll, Mike Stange, George Downing and Buzzy Trent—successfully cracked Waimea Bay and Sunset Beach, the nine-mile stretch between Haleiwa and Sunset Beach—commonly known as the North Shore—quickly became the proving ground for generations of surfers to come. It remains the site of prestigious contests, such as the Triple Crown of Surfing, where modern kings and queens are crowned.

Cover of *Vogue*'s December 1938 "cruise issue."
Waikiki Beach Boy and his *wahine* pupil, tandem
surfing on a redwood board. Roxy collection

Photo: Jim Russi

Makaha, Surf Mecca

In early times, Makaha (meaning "fierce") was considered a dangerous place, inhabited by an infamous band of robbers who lived deep in the valley and terrorized travelers. By the middle of the twentieth century, before Oahu's North Shore became the undisputed surfing Mecca of the world, Makaha had become Hawaii's acknowledged surfing crown jewel.

On the west and drier side of Oahu, Makaha offers a long, wide beach with ideal waves for surfers of any skill. Makaha waves break at one foot and at thirty feet. Many famous surfers have cut their teeth in Makaha's plentiful waves.

The early days of competition brought recognition as well as great fun to Makaha. Competitors were treated to a luau, night surfing with torches and searchlights, dancing to live bands on the beach and down-to-earth country hospitality. Makaha was a family beach, and remains so to this day.

When swells wrap around Kaena Point and roll down the coast to the shallow crescent bay that is Makaha, surfers enjoy long walls of water with a shallow bowl section waiting at the end of the ride. The challenge is to catch a wave coming off the point of the bay and ride it all the way through the bowl before it breaks.

When the surf breaks closer to shore, a fun, high-performance wave is created, along with the famous Makaha backwash, which forms a wave returning to sea after washing onto the steep beach. Surfers are often catapulted into the air when they collide with the backwash.

Although the Makaha International Surfing Championship has become an event of the past, Makaha is still the site of contests, including two popular amateur events, both founded about twenty-five years ago: Buffalo's Big Board Surfing Classic and Rell Sunn's Menehune Triple Lei of Surfing. These contests epitomize Aloha, the Hawaiian spirit of giving, through the sense of community they engender.

Buffalo's Big Board contest, named after Makaha's patriarch, Buffalo Keaulana, showcases longboarding, canoe surfing, tandem surfing, bodyboarding and bodysurfing. Keaulana has spent his entire life on this beach, and knows all its nuances. He ceremoniously rides the first wave to signal the start of the contest, which attracts renowned watermen and -women and their families from all over the Islands.

At the annual Menehune Contest, founded by Rell Sunn, another lifelong Makaha resident surfer who passed away in 1998, families come out to cheer on young boys and girls competing in bodyboarding, shortboarding and longboarding over a three-day period. Each participant receives a commemorative T-shirt and goodie bag. Every child who reaches a final receives a prize.

At both contests, the focus is on the fun of surfing and respect for the environment. It is ironic that once-fierce Makaha has become the site of such boundless Aloha.

1956 Makaha International program.
Roxy collection

Marge rode her Velzy balsawood board to win the Makaha
International in 1958. Photo: Marge Calhoun collection

Destiny of a Dynasty

Marjorie Booth Calhoun's love of the ocean is elemental and primal. Introduced by her parents to the salty realm as a baby, Marge Booth was immediately captivated. "They had to teach me to swim right away, because every time I got loose I'd head for the water," she says.

Marge Calhoun

Looking back, Calhoun says that going in the ocean was like going home. "The water was safe and curative," she adds. "If I had problems—the stress of dealing with all the stuff that life entails—I'd go out surfing and look back at the land, and I'd forget what was bothering me. I've never experienced fear in the water. I always wore a grin and had a tickle in my stomach."

Calhoun was born in Hollywood in the twenties when much of the area was dirt roads and orange groves. Her father worked in set production in the fledgling movie industry. Favorite family outings were to beaches of Venice, Santa Monica and Ocean Park. Blonde, five-foot-eight Calhoun could have been a Hollywood starlet, but her heart led her elsewhere. She took up competitive swimming and diving at a young age and was training for the 1940 Olympics when World War II broke out. Her competitive urges wouldn't be satisfied for more than a decade in the rollicking surf of California and Hawaii.

Calhoun's expertise led her to work as a water-stunt woman in movies and as a synchronized swimmer in a Las Vegas-style show called the Starlight Spectacular at California's Marineland aquarium.

She married her high school sweetheart, Tom Calhoun, and had two daughters, Carol (Candy) and Robin, before she discovered surfing. "I now realize that everything built up to surfing," she says. "I had no idea when I was young that surfing would be my destiny."

She first saw someone surf a wave while with Tom at the beach below Topanga Canyon, in the mid-fifties. "There were three guys out in the water: Matt Kivlin, Wally Reed and a guy named Percy. I was so excited. Tom, who loved scuba diving, turned to me and said, 'You know, Marge, you could do that.'"

That Christmas, Tom surprised her with a balsa-wood surfboard shaped by Joe Quigg, a friend from the construction business who would go on to become one of the most successful surfboard shapers of his era. "The first time I took the board out was at the Colony in Malibu," Calhoun remembers. "I stumbled down the cliff path to the sand and, much to my surprise, there was this diminutive, platinum-blonde girl on the beach with a surfboard. She was very friendly, took me under her wing and showed me how to get started."

The young girl was Darilyn Zanuck, daughter of the famous movie producer Darryl F. Zanuck. Zanuck and Calhoun became good friends and surfed together for several years. "When I first went out in the surf, Darilyn told me, 'Get in front of the whitewater and stand up.' I did, and when I went to stand up, I slipped and landed on my bottom facing sideways to the shore, my legs straight up in the air. But my board was trimmed to the wave and I rode it, laughing, all the way in. I got right back on and kept going."

Indeed, that was Calhoun's approach to life. Each time she faced a setback or challenge—such as divorce and raising her children alone—she got right back on and kept going. She focused her energy on raising her daughters, judging contests, surfing and promoting the sport. She was a cofounder and secretary of the U.S. Surfing Association (USSA), which mounted and won several campaigns to keep California beaches open to surfing during the sport's tumultuous growth years of the sixties.

Calhoun believes that "surfing makes you mentally healthy. It certainly kept a lot of young people out of trouble. Those who got up early and surfed before school, then surfed again after school, were too tired to get into mischief." She encouraged young people to surf, and girls to retain their femininity. "In the sixties, as surfing got more popular, more boys and girls headed to the surf. The boys didn't make the girls feel welcome in the water, so many of them felt they had to imitate the boys. I'd tell them that they didn't have to look like a gremmie, in baggy suits with uncombed hair. I never got hassled in the water. I was always polite and never antagonistic." But Calhoun had an advantage over the "gremmies." She had surfed the big waves with the famous pioneer surfers.

In 1958, she and her friend Eve Fletcher flew to Oahu to compete in the Makaha International contest. There, surfing greats George Downing, Buzzy Trent, Fred Hemmings and Fred Van Dyke became their mentors. Calhoun and Fletcher paid Van Dyke $100 to live in his panel truck for a month. In California a few years earlier, Trent had given Calhoun a lesson in eight-foot beach break at State Beach. In Hawaii he taught her how to survive wipeouts in big surf: relax, follow the bubbles to the top and bite the froth to get air. Calhoun, then in her thirties, won the 1958 Makaha contest riding a ten-foot balsa-wood board made for her by pioneer shaper and surfer Dale Velzy; the board is still in her possession and in pristine condition. She and Fletcher also surfed the hot spots of Oahu's North Shore, from Haleiwa to Sunset Beach. "I was always good in big surf. That's where I felt most comfortable, that's where I wanted to be. I was a big, strong woman. I loved the take off and that drop down the face of a big wave. It was so exhilarating."

Top: Marge and her father at the beach.
Photo: Marge Calhoun collection

Bottom: Body builder Russ Saunders,
Marge and Robin Calhoun, Muscle Beach,
1950s. Photo: Marge Calhoun collection.

She admired the Hawaiians and their love of the sea. "When the door of the airplane opened and the warm, fragrant air hit me, I realized I hadn't known anything like that existed. And I quickly realized that I was with people who feel like I do. They just adore the sea. I like their lore, everything about the Hawaiians." She returned home, vowing to take her daughters to Hawaii with her the next time. They finally went together in 1962, and again in 1963, when all three competed in the Makaha contest. "Candy had won the West Coast Championship in 1963, and part of the prize was a free trip to Hawaii to compete in the Makaha contest. That made it easier for me and Robin to go, too."

Her daughters followed her into the water, she says, "like ducklings," and also became accomplished waterwomen. Eldest daughter Candy was especially adept at bodysurfing, and fearlessly tackled the famous Newport Beach Wedge on days when the waves broke at eighteen to twenty feet. Marge, Candy and Robin often surfed together and became a common, if not famous, sight at surf spots and contests well into the sixties. Needless to say, for the girls surfing took precedence over all else. Calhoun still has a note Candy wrote at age thirteen in declaration of her independence from homemaking: "Right now the 'distaff' [role] doesn't intrigue me

The Calhouns at Makaha: Robin, Marge and
Candy. Photo: LeRoy Grannis

U.S. SURFBOARD CHAMPIONSHIPS AT HUNTINGTON BEACH ■ ■
winter preview/sunset beach and rincon●

at all because I'm all wrapped up in the sport of body surfing."

The Calhouns shared waves with the best surfers of the day, and left an indelible impression on many. California waterman and former world champion Mike Doyle recalls: "The warmest memories of my life are with the Calhouns. We surfed San Onofre during the day, and, if the swell was up, Candy and I bodysurfed in the evening at Brooks Street. Candy was like a seal. She liked being in the water more than on land. She rode surfboards, but she liked to be more in touch with the water. That's why she rode her Paipo board or bodysurfed. Less gravity, more sensual and intimate.

"All three had hair the color of amber honey, and skin golden and flawless. They were like Greek Goddesses, each one beautiful, and, together, overwhelming. My relationship with the girls was one of innocent play based on a background of the beach and surfing. With Marge, we had our fun in the ocean, but there was always an underlying respect between us about what was important. Although we never dared talk about it, we had great feelings for each other."

Calhoun admired her fellow surfers—male and female—and compliments them all. She describes Southern California surfer Linda Merrill as "the most graceful surfer I ever saw on a board." Hawaiian champion Anona Napoleon is "the sweetest." She admired Fred Van Dyke's sister, Gretchen, who had only one leg. "Somebody would carry her board to the water, then she'd paddle out and catch waves and ride them, balanced on one leg." She notes Shelley Merrick's "tenacity and beautiful competitive spirit." Betty Heldrich was "the most competent," having built her own house and dug her own swimming pool at Makaha. Lynne Boyer had "beautiful skill." Margo Oberg was "gutsy." At Rincon, Mary Monks was "the best. She'd ride screaming, 'It's my wave, it's my wave!' at the guys trying to drop in on her." Mike Doyle was the "Ironman." Jeff Clark, who pioneered Maverick's, the big-wave spot near Santa Cruz, is her friend and "hero." The list of Calhoun's admirees could go on indefinitely.

She talks about surfing at Malibu in the mid-sixties, when the waves had become crowded and guys were dropping in on her, cutting her off waves. "My friend Alan Malama, a big Hawaiian, said, 'Marge, get behind me on the wave and I'll pick them all off for you.' We'd catch a wave together and Alan would go in front of me on his big board, come up behind the surfers and literally pick them off their boards by the seat of their pants and toss them off the back of the

Top: Marge, Candy and Robin Calhoun grace the cover of *Surf Guide*, 1964.
Marge Calhoun collection

Bottom: Peter Cole and Marge Calhoun, winners of the 1958 Makaha International Surfing Championships. Photo: Marge Calhoun collection

wave. We did it for fun, but the guys got the message."

Calhoun loved every aspect of surfing. "I can remember getting wiped out and rolling around in the water, laughing to myself. I always knew who was the boss. The ocean doesn't care whether or not you ride the waves. There is no 'conquering,' other than yourself."

She sold her extensive quiver of longboards to young and aspiring surfers in her neighborhood at prices far below market value. "It's good that someone gets use out of them," she says. Now retired from surfing and in her seventies ("I did it as long as I could"), she often goes down to the shore near her Northern California home to watch the new generation of wave riders.

What advice does Calhoun offer youngsters? "I tell them that surfing is simple and good for the soul. All you need is a surfboard and a bar of wax. God provides the rest."

Marge shows her stuff at Makaha, 1962.
Photo: LeRoy Grannis

Eve Fletcher Rips

Eve Fletcher and her parents moved from the East Coast to California's San Fernando Valley in 1937, when Eve was ten. "We came on the boat through the Panama Canal," says Fletcher. "My parents joined the Westport Beach Club, where I swam competitively. My dad would take me down to the ocean and take me out in waves that I thought were huge, but probably weren't. I loved it."

Fletcher didn't start surfing until 1957, when she was thirty. She joined the San Onofre Surf Club and also frequented other spots such as Malibu and Rincon. She worked at Disney Studios as an inker and then supervised its Ink and Paint Department. She paddled with the actor John Sheffield (who played "Boy" in several *Tarzan* mov-

ies). Sheffield gave Fletcher her first board. "It was about ten feet long. I used it at Malibu to practice paddling."

When she started surfing, she says, "The fellows didn't really like us out there, but they respected you when you finally learned. I remember when I was learning, Warnie Miller would come up to me and bump my shins with his surfboard. Then I got good and did it back to him and he was nice to me after that."

At San Onofre, Fletcher met Calhoun, Alice Petersen, Liz Irwin and many of the other San-O regulars. "When Marge and I went to Hawaii, I had only been surfing about a year," she says. "We didn't know anything about the place. But, after we met everyone and

Eve riding San Onofre, 1999.
Photo: Jim Russi

they could see that we were serious about surfing, we had a wonderful time."

Back in California, Fletcher hit the waves every weekend. San Onofre was her favorite. "We'd camp at the beach, have potluck barbecues and bonfires in the fire pits. By some process of natural selection, the beachgoers divided up into three groups. The south beach set would pour all different kinds of booze in a big bucket and mix it up. The north beach group was called the 'martini and diaphragm' set. Otis Chandler and those people—they'd have catered meals. I was part of the middle beach crowd. I'd be with Liz Irwin and her kids. Most of us middle-beachers drank beer or wine, and not very much of it."

In 1966, a group of out-of-town surfers came to San Onofre to practice for the world championships in San Diego. "Liz, Alice and I were out in the water, and there was the most wonderful south swell. It was coming in beautifully, gorgeous shape, ten feet and bigger. I haven't seen it that good since. I caught a wave and lost my board. A sixteen-year-old Aussie boy paddled it back out to me. We surfed some more, and later I saw him on shore. He came over to me and said, 'Wow, I can't wait to get home and tell everyone that all the old ladies here surf!' I was only in my late thirties."

Now in her early seventies, the slender, five-foot-three Fletcher still surfs San Onofre several times a week. She declares, "The greatest thing about surfing is that you learn so much about the ocean, the birds, the por-

poises. You forget all your problems. You love everyone." She sometimes heads out with her friend, fifty-four-year-old Pattie Clover, who moved to Minnesota five years ago but travels to California regularly to surf. Fletcher rides an eight-foot-six board made by Steve Boehne.

Fletcher usually surfs San Onofre to be among friends. She is not interested in other scenes. "I just go down in the mornings. It's getting so crowded that I avoid the weekends. Now that I'm retired, I can say, 'Don't these people work?'"

The video documentary, "Surfing for Life" prominently features Fletcher. She traveled to Haleiwa on Oahu's North Shore in fall 1999 for the premiere. "It was wonderful to see our old friends Fred Van Dyke, Peter Cole and Rabbit Kekai. I hadn't seen them in forty-three years. I stayed at Vicki Heldrich's house [Heldrich won the Makaha championship in 1957]. We didn't surf because there weren't any waves."

Fletcher intends to surf until she drops. "I hate to admit it, but I know I don't have the strength and stamina I used to have. I can remember being held under at Makaha for a long time and wondering when I would get a breath. I don't think I could do that now."

But, she adds, "I don't think you can be too old to be stoked."

Eve Fletcher and her 8'6" Infinity surfboard. Photo: Andrea Gabbard

The first *Gidget* movie starred Sandra Dee.
Roxy collection

Gidget

She didn't rip, shred or go on surf safaris. She simply pestered her way in among a bunch of Malibu regulars and kept a diary. From that diary grew the Gidget phenomenon. First, her father, screenwriter Frederick Kohner, wrote the book, *Gidget*, in 1957. The book spawned three Gidget movies, the first in 1959, and inspired more than two dozen "beach party" movies throughout the sixties. *Gidget* ignited the imaginations of countless teenagers and introduced the word "bitchin" (spelled "bitchen" in the book) into their lingo. To the chagrin of surfers suddenly having to share waves with the hordes, and to the delight of those who would create businesses out of surfing, Gidget lured inland America to the beach.

The girl who started this craze was an exuberant, five-foot-one Jewish brunette from Brentwood, California, named Kathy Kohner. Today, she is Kathy Kohner Zuckerman, happily married to Marvin (a professor from the Bronx) for the past thirty-five years, mother of Phil and David and grandmother of baby Ruby. For the last ten years, Zuckerman has been a hostess at the Broadway Bar & Grill in Santa Monica. Her business card reads: "Gidget."

In the summer of 1956, fifteen-year-old Kathy was feeling displaced. The family had just returned from living in Europe for a year, and she had not yet reconnected with her friends. "My contemporaries planned to spend their summer going to movies in Westwood," she says. "My mother said, 'No, no, no, that's not healthy. It's a beautiful day, this is Southern California, you're going to the beach to get some fresh air.'"

Kohner's mother had friends at the Colony in Malibu, so Kohner elected to go there. She asked to be dumped at "the Pit," a spot on the sand near a concrete wall where the surfers hung out. Although her mother had pushed Kohner to the beach, she never saw her daughter surf. "She'd sit at the Colony with her friends. It was my father who would walk down to see what was going on with his little girl. My sister would come down, too."

Kohner was already somewhat familiar with surfing. Her mother, who drove a Ford jalopy with a

Kohner surfing Malibu's inside break.
Photo: Warren Miller

rumble seat, often gave neighborhood boys Buzzy Trent and Matt Kivlin a lift to Malibu. They'd stick their surfboards in the rumble seat and Kohner would ride along. "Buzzy lived on the corner of San Vincente and Seventh. Matt lived on Westgate and Sunset." Trent would later migrate to the big waves of Oahu's North Shore and become a legend as one of the first among the "men who ride mountains," the elite cadre of surfers brave and skillful enough to ride waves twenty feet and higher. Kivlin became a renowned surfboard shaper and Malibu surf stylist whose casual, polished style was copied by the young generation of surfers who ushered the sport into the sixties.

At Malibu, Kohner ingratiated herself with the guys, as she put it, "somewhat like in the movie. I'd bring them sandwiches."

She describes them and their quirks: "Some of the surfers sat in the Pit, then there were some that sat away from the Pit. I was never quite sure if there was rivalry between the two groups. Tubesteak (Terry Tracey, the inspiration for "Kahoona" in *Gidget*) lived in a shack. He got his nickname from eating roasted hot dogs for every meal. I was very curious about this, a young man living in a shack on the beach."

Kathy "Gidget" Kohner at Malibu.
Photo: Kathy Kohner Zuckerman collection

Moondoggie, the fictional Gidget's love interest, did exist but he was not Kohner's. "I actually had a crush on Bill Jenson, who was a gorgeous blond, blue-eyed surfer boy," says Kohner. The crush went unrequited. "Moondoggie was actually Billy Al Bengston, a famous artist living in Venice, California. The reason they called Billy Al 'Moondoggie' is because he'd come out of the water and shake his head and water would fly off his beard, like a dog shaking off."

The Malibu regulars included now-famous surfers Mickey Dora, Mickey Muñoz and Mike Doyle, all of whom gradually warmed up to Kohner and—paying her the ultimate male compliment—teased her and played pranks. "One day, somebody said, 'You're a midget and a girl—you're a Gidget!' Tubesteak likes to claim that he thought of it. It might have been Jerry Hurst, or Golden Boy. Anyway, the name stuck."

It was a very innocent time. "Most of the guys were going to college. This was the summer holiday for them. There was nothing going on to cause me any sort of alarm. I never heard about drugs, I knew nothing about sex then. I was never sexually or romantically involved with the guys on the beach." Hopefully, this revelation does not disappoint Gidget fans.

Kohner bought her first surfboard at Malibu from fifteen-year-old Mike Doyle. "I gave him thirty-five dollars for it. The board had a totem pole design on it and was called the 'Totem Pole Board.' I don't know what happened to it after I sold it." Doyle's mother painted totem poles on all his surfboards when he was young. Today, surfer/shaper Robert August still makes a Doyle model with a totem pole design.

Kohner learned to surf by imitation; there were no classes or mentors to guide her. "I put my body on the board, started paddling and watched what the other surfers were doing. I never ventured to the second break. I stayed in at the first break. It didn't take long to learn, and I was very pleased with myself. There was a great sense of, 'I can do it too, guys!' At that time, I didn't understand gender issues. I just thought, 'I'm Kathy, and I can do it.'"

Fascinated by the subculture that she had stumbled upon in the Pit, she started telling her father stories and reading to him from her diaries. Sensing a winner, he wrote *Gidget* and sold it to the movies six weeks later. "The agent who read the finished book exclaimed: 'You've got a sequel here, you've got a movie, and you've got a television series. You and your wife can just enjoy life.'" Which is exactly what they did.

Their daughter's fame followed her to college in Oregon, where some of the boys were too intimidated to ask her for a date. "I'd hear them say, 'There goes that Gidget girl,'" she remembers. She stopped surfing in 1960. "I think the surfing was a rite of passage for me. I became interested in other things and met my husband, who had no idea what the surfing world was all about."

Gidget, published in 1957, lured inland
America to the beach. Roxy collection

35

Kohner hints that she might get back out in the water for her sixtieth birthday in January 2001. "I get invited to longboard contests," she says. "People are interested to know that there really was a Gidget at Malibu. It's nice that today's surf culture is embracing me. Most people think of Sandra Dee or Sally Field when they think of Gidget."

One person will always remember the real Gidget. "When I went away to college in Corvallis, Oregon, my first boyfriend was a boy from Maui," Kohner recalls. "Last May, he showed up at the restaurant where I work and told me that I had always been so important to him. After forty years! He said to him I had always been 'that Gidget girl,' and he wanted to tell me that he loved me. He now lives in Perth, Australia. His cousin was with him and told me, 'We've always known about the Gidget girl.'"

Kohner at the shack where Tubesteak lived.
Photo: Kathy Kohner Zuckerman collection

The Women of Malibu

By Jeff Duclos

Few people know about the contributions the women of Malibu made to surfing more than fifty years ago. On revolutionary surfboards designed by Joe Quigg and Matt Kivlin, three women in particular—Vicki (Flaxman) Williams, Aggie (Bane) Quigg and Robin Grigg—set a hard edge towards the evolution of high performance surfing on the waves of postwar Malibu. "They may not be recognized as pioneers today," notes former Malibu regular and big-wave riding legend Ricky Grigg, who is also Robin's brother. "But, when you think back, they were the ones."

Vicki, Aggie, Robin, Claire Cassidy, Darilyn Zanuck and a few other young women had been surfing Malibu waves long before "Gidget" arrived on the scene. And these women knew they were not the first. If they needed inspiration, they found it in Mary Ann (Hawkins) Morrisey, who had ridden Malibu, and ridden it well, more than a decade earlier.

Featured in Doc Ball's book, *California Surfriders 1946,* Morrisey possessed a movie star's figure and looks. From the late thirties through the forties, she was grace personified in the water. Like many top lifeguards of the time, she worked in Hollywood as a stunt person (and often would double for actress and swimmer Esther Williams). Morrisey eventually moved to Hawaii, where she created a swim school for babies at the Hilton Hawaiian Village. Robin Grigg eventually moved to the Islands herself and taught with Morrisey.

In 1943, when Grigg was nine, she moved with her mother and her brother, Ricky, to a large beach house on Santa Monica's Muscle Beach. "I used to hang out at the lifeguard tower and the lifeguards got to know me. Tommy Zahn took a liking to me and I became his little protégé." Zahn built her a ten-foot balsa-wood surfboard. "It had a big square tail and weighed about sixty pounds." The board was an early version of Joe Quigg's ground-breaking Girl Boards that followed.

Grigg first visited Malibu in the late forties—when surfers had to sneak through a hole in a chainlink fence to get to the beach. She was fifteen. "I was just a little gremmie riding along with the big guys," she says. "We'd collect Coke bottles and turn them in at the market across the street for two cents each and get a loaf of bread and some mustard. That's what we ate for the day. In those days, there wasn't a group of kids that got together and went out surfing. It was an older crowd. I got to tag along because I happened to live behind the lifeguard station."

Aggie Bane and Robin Grigg had been friends since Sunday school. One day during the winter of 1950 at State Beach, the girls ran into Matt Kivlin and Joe Quigg. "Aggie caught one look at Joe and she was in love," recalls Grigg.

Vicki Flaxman didn't start surfing until the following summer. "Aggie was going with Joe by then and he made her a board, so I ordered one. I'd only been surfing once or twice before that." She progressed quickly.

"The thing that was unique about Aggie, Claire and Vicki," says Joe Quigg, "was that they went out on those boards, and, in a couple of weeks, they were standing up and coming across the face of the wave at Malibu." Each girl soon developed her own approach to surfing, Quigg adds: "Aggie was just out there for fun. Vicki was a little more athletic and aggressive. In a couple months, she learned to surf better than most men."

The key to this advance in performance, according to Quigg, was the combination of rail and tail rocker blended end to end. Up until then, surfboards were stick straight, like planks. Quigg's Girl Boards curved gently from nose to tail. "These were the first boards that were light and had rail rocker," he says. "Before that, all the boards had straight decks and straight rails. When I rockered the whole board, especially the tail, that let a person change direction instantly. That's what helped Vicki look better than most men out there, because they got those boards first. And, oh, the men were jealous. A lot of people don't want to admit that, but many big name Malibu guys did not like women out there looking that good." But most accepted and encouraged the girls.

According to Vicki Flaxman Williams, "The guys at Malibu were really nice to us, with a couple of exceptions. When we first learned, there were only two breaks at Malibu: a mid-break closer to shore and the point. We learned at mid-break and the guys would let us in the waves." Aggie adds, "We'd be surfing and there'd be a guy beside us and he'd say, 'Come on! Get on board.' And we'd step from our board onto his. We did a lot of playing."

Each woman would paint her name and a special design on her Girl Board, and the boards eventually became known by name (i.e., the Aggie Board, the Vicki Board). One that became particularly well known was the Di-Di Board, shaped by Matt Kivlin for his girlfriend, Diane. "Hers was one of the first really light balsawood boards," recalls Robin. "It had

Vicki Flaxman and Robin Grigg with their Girl Board. Photo: Joe Quigg collection

a scoop nose. I fell in love with that board and, at some point, somehow I acquired it. I took it up to Stanford with me when I first started going there. A friend took it to Santa Cruz one day and it got broken in half. I was so pissed, because that, to me, was the ultimate surfboard."

In 1950, the women joined Kivlin, Quigg and others on a surf trip down the coast. They made all the stops along the way—Salt Creek, San Onofre, Sunset Cliffs and Baja. "Everybody we met was kind of dazzled because we had these balsa boards," recalls Williams.

The seeds of the design revolution had been spread. The girls were maturing and starting to move on. Bane and Grigg began working as lifeguards. "But not at the beach," Grigg adds. "In those days, they didn't let girls work the beach. We worked at the municipal pools. Aggie and I both lifeguarded and taught swimming. We made better money than most girls could make working in the dime store or whatever. I was able to save up enough to pay my way through college. My Malibu days essentially stopped on a regular basis around the summer of '52.

"Almost all of us from that time went to college," Grigg continues. "We all had other things going on in our lives besides surfing. Surfing was something we did that pulled us together and set us apart."

"Basically, my life changed," says Williams of the same end to her Malibu experience. "I had a baby in 1957. I was teaching school. My husband didn't surf. It became so much of a hassle."

Bane married Joe Quigg in 1950 and continued to be near the water. In addition to surfing, she launched herself into canoeing. "Patty O'Keefe, Vicki and I were on a championship canoe paddling team in Hawaii."

Thanks to Tommy Zahn, who taught her all the finer points of paddling, Grigg went on to compete for years as a champion paddler. "I never lost a race, even when I came over here to Hawaii," says Grigg, who now owns a ranch on the Big Island and continues her practice as a physical therapist.

"When the idea of *Gidget* came along, the writer, of course, picked his daughter. You can't blame him for that," observes Ricky Grigg. "But the idea of it was the young girl at Malibu. That could have been Robin, or Vicki or Aggie—or all three of them."

The youngest surfer to win the Makaha International: Linda Benson, age 15.
Photo: LeRoy Grannis

The Making of a Champion

Linda Benson

In the fifties, Southern California's Moonlight Beach was a paradise of warm sand, gentle surf and, most important, uncrowded waves. That's where Linda Benson grew up. "In 1955, my older brother Charlie was seventeen and I was eleven," Benson recalls. "I used to stand on the cliffs above the beach and watch him surf with his friends. I was fascinated. I thought it was the neatest thing I had ever seen."

Gradually, Benson went down on the beach to watch. Then she started wading out in the water to retrieve lost boards. In no time, she was paddling the boards back out to the surfers. "One day, one of the guys let me try to catch a wave on his board. I stood up, and from that time on I was a real pest. Always asking to use a board. The guys were great, they'd let me use their boards. Most of the time, they'd have to carry the board down to the water for me, because it was so heavy, but I persisted."

By the following summer, the twelve-year-old Benson had talked her father into buying her an eight-foot-six, water-logged and battered balsawood board for twenty dollars. Unsure of her ability and concerned about his daughter spending her entire summer at the beach among the boys, Benson's father first consulted with the local lifeguard, John Elwell, who responded: "Go ahead and let her get the board. She already surfs better than most of the guys."

Benson never looked back. She surfed all she could, and she ate up everything in print about surfing, especially women's surfing. "When I heard that there was a book out about a girl surfer in Malibu named Gidget, I couldn't wait to read it. In 1958, there was a story on Marge Calhoun winning the women's division of the Makaha International contest in Hawaii. I cut out the photo and hung it on my bedroom wall for inspiration. Later, Marge would become a comfort to me throughout my career. Through her judging and contest organizing, she was always very friendly and caring."

In 1959, the first U.S. Championships were held in Huntington Beach—it eventually turned into the largest contest in the U.S. Benson entered and won on a new foam board made for her by Dale Velzy.

She immediately set her sights on Makaha. "Velzy would send a small group of men to Hawaii each year to compete at Makaha. I asked him if I could go, too. He thought about it for a while, then made me a deal. He said he'd send me over there if I'd pay my way back. Luckily, my father was willing to foot the bill. John Elwell arranged for me to stay with Hobie and Sharon Alter [Hobie Alter was the founder of Hobie Surfboards] on the

North Shore. My parents trusted them."

In Hawaii, the surfing community protected the five-foot-two Benson. "At fifteen, I was the youngest surfer ever to enter the Makaha contest. Going there was like a dream come true. The only images I had seen of Hawaii were like those you see in travel agencies, people on six-foot waves at a surf spot called Canoes. I was on my own, but everyone took care of me. It was a time of real innocence and joy."

Benson spent a few weeks before the contest getting familiar with the waves. "All the competitors stayed in or around Makaha, and we'd all surf together, almost every day. At the time, my main competition was Joey Hamasaki, Robin Grigg, Anona Naone and some other Hawaiian girls." The day of the contest, the waves were breaking at about five feet, "good enough to have fun in," says Benson, modestly, knowing how many contests end up in mushy two-foot waves. "My heart was in my throat." Her anxiety didn't show in her surfing: she won.

Mike Doyle, who also competed at Makaha, remembers the event: "Linda was the hot-dogger of the women. She had incredible wave judgment and literally ripped the waves apart."

Benson returned home famous. "I landed at Lindbergh Field in San Diego. My family, my best surfing friends and the San Diego newspaper were there."

Few know that while in Hawaii for that contest, Benson became the first woman to surf Waimea Bay, a spot on the North Shore famous for monstrous winter surf. "It wasn't a huge day by Waimea standards. Some of the waves were breaking around eighteen feet," she recalls. "I got a real nervous stomach, but I was determined to try it. I borrowed the smallest 'gun' I could find, about a ten-foot-six board, and started paddling out. John Severson, who founded *Surfer* magazine that year, was on the beach taking pictures. He said, 'You're crazy,' but he followed me into the water.

"We saw Fred Van Dyke get wiped out. He lost his board. He popped up, and half his board popped up beside him. The other piece came up halfway across the bay. I sat out there for about two hours before I tried for

Waxing up for Makaha.
Photo: John Elwell

a wave. I can remember the steepness, the speed of the wave and the spray of the water in my face from the wind. It nearly blinds you. I felt the drop and hoped that I could stay on. The wave was maybe fifteen feet."

She also rode Sunset Beach and regarded it as more intimidating than Waimea. "The surf breaks all over the place, the current is strong and it's a longer paddle out to the waves. It had started to rain, and I suddenly realized that I was out there by myself. I really wanted to paddle in, but I was afraid. I had heard stories about the North Shore and how fast it could close out. After a while, I saw someone paddling out. As he got closer, I realized it was Ricky Grigg. We caught a wave together and came in."

Although she had felt fear, other feelings took precedence. "Asking me today about fear and asking a fifteen-year-old are two different things. Then, I wanted to be able to say that I had ridden Waimea Bay and Sunset. I was scared and probably didn't use the best judgment. My ego led the way. Today, I understand how fear plays a big role in judgment. It's the inside beacon that guides us. I think you have to be able to take a risk in whatever you do or you're not going to gain anything. But with the ocean, you have to be careful." She pauses to smile. "I don't want to be towed into a massive wave and I'll never go out at Waimea again."

During the ten years following her win at Makaha, Benson won a total of five U.S. championships. She also worked as a stunt double in several surf movies, including *Gidget Goes Hawaiian*. She relates: "In 1963, the movie company paid each stunt surfer three-hundred-and-fifty dollars a week, plus I got an extra hundred-dred each time I went in the water, which sometimes was three or four times a day. I felt rich!"

Despite her fame, Benson never thought of herself as a professional athlete. "Surfing was something I loved and happened to be good at. There was no 'tour.' The contests were just something we did because we enjoyed the sport."

Benson faced the best women surfers of the day. "Joey Hamasaki, Jericho Poppler and Joyce Hoffman were all great competitors, but Joyce was an especially huge threat," says Benson. "And then, toward the end of the sixties, Margo (Godfrey) Oberg came on. She was about twelve and already a beautiful surfer. She really gave Joyce a run."

In the mid-sixties, Benson joined United Airlines as a flight attendant and today, at fifty-six, is a senior flight attendant. She used to keep a surfboard in the beach lockup in Honolulu. "I was surfing Queens one day knowing that I had to

Benson was one of the first surfers, man or woman, to ride the nose. Photo: John Severson

43

be showered and ready to go on my flight by one o'clock. I was showering off at Kuhio Beach at like 12:30 p.m. Six feet at Queens and I hated to leave!"

Benson modeled her surfing style after the "Little Man On Wheels," Dewey Weber. A revolutionary surfboard shaper and surfer, Weber had perfected a style called "hot-dogging," which involves performing multiple maneuvers on and with a surfboard, including cutting back and forth on the wave and walking to the nose of the board and hanging five or ten toes over the edge. Benson was among the first surfers, male or female, to "walk the nose." (Since Joe Quigg introduced the first Girl Board, surfers and shapers had discovered that a certain degree of rocker—or curve—in the surfboard, especially in the tail, enabled them to walk to the nose without the board flipping up in back. The combination of forward speed and water bending up along the curve of the tail created suction and kept the tail down.)

"I think I was definitely among the first to start moving around on the board, doing more difficult moves," she says. "We also started learning about timing and judgment. By 1959, I was riding a foam board. I rode a nine-foot board at Makaha. Today, I ride an eight-two or eight-six. Both are featherlight compared to my old boards. They're also faster and more maneuverable."

She passed her most memorable surfing day with Weber. It was the first time she had ever surfed Trestles, so named for the train trestle above the beach, part of a U.S. Marine base near Oceanside, California. Surfers would sneak into Trestles and surf until the Marines chased them off.

"It was one of those beautiful, glassy days, with a slight, warm Santa Ana wind. The waves were five and six feet, perfect. I paddled out and watched Dewey for a while. He was so hot. I started surfing and it was *so* good. Soon, the Marines rolled up in their tanks and started practice-firing on the beach—not at us, of course, but it was the usual warning to clear out. Everyone else went in but me and Dewey. I figured, 'I'll go in when he goes in.' The Marines were on the beach, and he and I had a super day of surfing. At the end of the day, we were escorted off the beach by tanks."

In retrospect, she adds, "It was a heady time. You'd know just about every car that had a surfboard in it, up and down the coast. The camaraderie among the surfers was great."

It was also the wild and woolly sixties and, like many in the surfing community, Benson was not immune to the pull of the party scene. Although she didn't shy away from waves, and earned plenty of accolades for her surfing ability, on land Benson continually battled an overwhelming sense of inadequacy. As she says, "I was

Official program, 1969 U.S. Surfing Championships,
Huntington Beach, featured Benson on the cover.
Courtesy Linda Benson collection

really shy and didn't feel like I fit in. I thought alcohol helped. At one time, I felt that if I couldn't drink and have fun with people, my life would be over." She finally confronted her demons and brought her life back into balance. She's been sober for twenty years.

After our interview on a sunny day in January 2000, we dropped in at Swami's Café on Coast Highway just above the famous Swami's surf break. The girls at the counter saw us admiring a photo on the wall of Benson at Makaha, and instantly put two and two together: "Is that you?" they asked. "Will you sign the photo?" Benson happily complied.

Benson recently moved from Manhattan Beach to a small town inland from Encinitas, to be close to the beaches where she grew up. Craving elbow room and serenity, she chose an eight-acre parcel with a rambling ranch house—and an avocado grove. Today, in addition to being a senior flight attendant with United, she also is an avocado and commercial flower farmer. "I knew nothing about this when I first moved in," she says, "but I find that I love learning about growing things."

Surfing is still her favorite pastime. "Surfing is one of the cleanest, purest forms of art and self expression." She adds, "I hope to do it as long as I'm alive." She is often recognized at Southern California breaks such as Cardiff, Swami's and Moonlight Beach. "I see lots of old friends at Cardiff in the summer when both longboarders and older surfers are out. Some of the young kids also know me and talk to me."

She and Joyce Hoffman are good friends and sometimes surf together—for fun. Benson laughs, "We'd *never* have called each other to go surfing when we were competing."

Legendary rivals, now friends. Joyce Hoffman and Linda Benson, 1998. Photo: Elizabeth Pepin

The Art of Tandem Surfing

The beauty and grace of tandem surfing was introduced by Duke Kahanamoku and Waikiki beach boys in the twenties. In surfing exhibitions around the world, Kahanamoku would ask a woman to step forward from the crowd of onlookers and ride a wave with him. At home in Hawaii, beach boys took tourist girls out for rides on their surfboards. During the first half of this century, many promotional postcards and brochures for Hawaii tourism depicted tandem surfers at Waikiki. At that time, the surfers either stood together on the board, woman in front, or the woman perched atop the man's shoulders. As the art of tandem surfing became more popular, more intricate maneuvers were developed.

During a trip to Hawaii in 1931, legendary surfers Pete Peterson and Lorrin Harrison discovered tandem surfing and brought it home to California. By the following year, they were tandem surfing in Malibu and Corona del Mar and attracting others to the sport. By the fifties, many other leading West Coast male surfers were riding tandem, including Walter Hoffman, Mike Doyle, Mickey Munoz, Hobie Alter and Don Hansen. In Hawaii, Fred Hemmings and Rabbit Kekai helped make the sport more visible.

For some women, being a tandem surfing partner meant that you could enjoy the thrill of riding a wave without actually knowing how to surf. For others, tandem riding was simply an extension of their love of surfing. Many top women competitors, including Joyce Hoffman, Linda Benson and Marge Calhoun, enjoyed tandem surfing.

Tandem surfing came naturally to Linda Merrill, who grew up in a surfing family in Southern California. Her mother gave her ballet lessons ("To make me trip more gracefully," she says) and her father, who was one of the founders of the San Onofre Surf Club, gave her tandem lessons. By ten, she had her own surfboard. "The first time I ever surfed tandem in a contest was in 1959 or 1960 with Bobby Ah Choy. I was fifteen," she recalls. "In 1963, Mike Doyle and I went to Hawaii and won the Makaha contest." While most tandem riders went straight off on a wave, Doyle and Merrill, with their combined expertise, would actually turn and surf the wave. The pair toured New York, Philadelphia and Washington, D.C., showing surf movies and promoting the sport. Today, Merrill lives on the central coast of California and often surfs Rincon with her son, Kevin. The two have not yet ridden tandem.

In the early sixties, Barrie (Algaw) Boehne got her start in tandem surfing on Muscle Beach as an acrobat. Algaw,

Linda Merrill and Mike Doyle, tandem champions.
Photo: LeRoy Grannis

only five feet tall and eighty-nine pounds, would stand on one end of a teeter board as two big men jumped onto the other end, catapulting her as high as the palm trees. She did back gainers and flips before the men caught her. One day, Pete Peterson visited Muscle Beach, looking for a new tandem partner, and happened to see Algaw flying through the air.

She quickly agreed to become Peterson's tandem partner, even though she could neither surf nor swim a stroke. "In those days, there was a requirement that the girl had to weigh half the man's weight," she explains. "Pete weighed two hundred pounds, so to meet the requirement, he put weight belts on me. The drawback was that, when we lost our surfboard, I would sink. He'd have to swim me in." In 1966, Peterson and Algaw won fourteen tandem events in a row, including the U.S. Championships, the Makaha International and the World Contest in San Diego.

In 1967, Algaw teamed up with Steve Boehne, a tandem surfer and friend of Peterson's. Boehne was quick to discover Algaw's acrobatic talents and together they took tandem surfing to a new level of technical difficulty by inventing and naming many new lifts. These lifts, including the High Stag, High Reverse Stag, Front Angel, Arrow and Helicopter, have become favorites for tandem teams the world over.

Their tandem partnership produced an enduring marriage of more than thirty years, a successful business (Infinity Surfboards, Inc.), two sons and a garage full of tro-

phies. They have taught their repertoire of lifts to dozens of tandem teams in California, Hawaii, France, England and South America. Each year, they journey to the Biarritz Surf Festival in France to give tandem surfing exhibitions. And in 1999, they traveled to Noosa Head, Australia, to defend their world tandem title.

It's not the winning that matters any more, says Barrie Boehne, who learned to swim and single surf years ago. "Doing radical maneuvers on a wave while being held up in the air by my partner and husband, doing a beautiful lift and feeling the wind on my face is a very thrilling experience."

Top: Practice makes perfect. The Boehnes on 19th Street, Newport Beach, ca 1970s. Courtesy Boehne collection

Bottom: Barrie and Steve Boehne, tandem team in and out of the water since 1967. Photo: LeRoy Grannis

47

The Athlete

Joyce Hoffman hails from a surfing family. Her father, Walter, and Uncle Philip ("Flippy") Hoffman surfed Malibu in the forties and pioneered big-wave surfing in Hawaii in the fifties. Her cousin Marty cut his teeth on North Shore monsters. Her sister Dibi and brother-in-law Herbie Fletcher—surf shop owner, filmmaker and entrepreneur—raised the surf aerialists Christian and Nathan Fletcher. One could hardly grow up in such a family and not surf.

Joyce Hoffman

Joyce Hoffman almost did. "I started going to the beach with my mom and dad when I was about ten," she recalls. "We'd go down to San Onofre and I'd climb around the hills, catch lizards, build forts, do everything but surf. We'd go to Killer Dana so that my dad could surf there, and I'd play in the sand."

Until she was a teenager, Hoffman competed in other sports, such as track and field and tennis. In 1960, when she was thirteen, the family moved to Capistrano Beach. "You could literally step out the front door and be on the beach," says Hoffman. "There was a surf spot there, and it was convenient to surf, so I started doing it, but only because it was convenient."

Hoffman was a natural athlete and knew she would pursue some sport professionally. She just couldn't decide which one. "I wanted to compete. For a while, I thought tennis might be it. Billie Jean King was starting out, and tennis was getting more coverage. Then I learned to ski and thought, 'Hmm, I could go to the Olympics.' My parents were very supportive and willing to help me, send me to a camp, whatever, if I could just decide."

In 1960, surfing didn't have much of a competitive foundation. "I knew there were contests, but there was no professional tour," says Hoffman. "I was planning on being the best I could be, and I was assuming it would be something like 'the best in the world.' I was a heck of an athlete and I knew I would take whatever sport it was as far as it could go. I kept thinking that surfing wasn't going to give me far enough to go."

Then she fell in love—with surfing. What started out simply as a convenient pastime turned into a passion. "Surfing gave me such a wonderful, exhilarating feeling. I loved the fact that it was just you, you didn't have to depend on somebody else to do this sport. So, I started looking at surfing more seriously."

Of course, her father was extremely supportive. Joyce gave up all other sports and focused solely on surfing. "I set my sights on being the best in the world," she says. "At the time, it was a very small pond, but I was going to be the biggest fish in that pond."

Opposite: Joyce Hoffman at Makaha, 1960s.
Photo: LeRoy Grannis

Her first contest was at Doheny State Beach in Dana Point. She entered the tandem event with her father, also known for his competitive bent. "That was the first and last time we ever competed in tandem," says Hoffman. "Because I was damned if I was going to have him telling me whether we were taking this wave or that wave and whether we were going right or left. We won, though."

The next contest she entered was held at the San Clemente Pier. She won there, too, and then there was no stopping her. Hoffman won the Makaha International in 1964 and then took five world titles between 1966 and 1971. She also became the first woman to surf the notorious and dangerous spot on the North Shore known as Pipeline, where waves form in shallow water over a menacing bed of sharp coral. The name "Pipeline" describes the tube formed by the curling, hollow wave, which breaks extremely fast, often catching the rider and smashing him against the coral. The ultimate ride is achieved by streaking across the wave inside the tube and emerging in the blast of spray created by the force of the breaking wave. Hoffman reached this nirvana—then had to be rescued from the riptide by Phil Edwards, the acknowledged best surfer of the day.

"The only reason I had gone out there was because Bud Browne was filming and I wanted to be recognized as the first woman to ride Pipeline," Hoffman recalls. "Thank God Bud got it on film. Then I lost my board. The rip was running like the Colorado River. I got caught in it and couldn't get out. My mom asked Phil to paddle

out and get me. Not a story I relish, but at least if you're going to be rescued, be rescued by your hero. Phil was my mentor in surfing. He was the one I wanted to emulate in style."

That was probably the last time Hoffman had to be rescued. Her star ascended just as surfing was attracting the attention of the masses, including mainstream media such as *Life, Teen, Seventeen* and *Sports Illustrated*. Hoffman attracted big-time sponsors—Leyland-Triumph, Bonne Bell, Catalina Swimwear and Hobie Surfboards. Honda even sent her a motorcycle. "They all paid just a token amount of money," Hoffman explains, "and gave me lots of product. After the 1966 World Championships, I took a trip around the world, and Triumph sponsored me with cars everywhere I went. The sponsors would tie me into their advertising in one way or another."

Hoffman's classic style, at Makaha, 1960s.
Photo: LeRoy Grannis

Hoffman trained like an athlete and is still trim and muscular. "Surfers weren't taken that seriously when I first started," she says. "The party reputation of the sport was well earned and well deserved. But I approached it like I would have any other sport. I made sure I surfed a minimum of two to four hours a day. I also ran and did weight training. I paddled in paddling competitions—there were lots of those held by lifeguard associations. I entered tandem paddling events with Mike Doyle.

"Because of this, I have always maintained that I don't know if I was the best surfer during those years, but I was the best trained, the best prepared and the best competitor. And that's why I won consistently."

Doyle offers this observation: "Joyce was a real competitor. It wasn't about soul surfing, it was about winning. I liked that in her. She has always had a no-bullshit approach to everything. You knew where you stood with Joyce, and if you weren't sure she would tell you."

Hoffman tells a story about the time she gave young Jericho Poppler a ride to a contest in Santa Cruz and Poppler beat her. "I wouldn't speak to her the entire way home. At least I took her home and didn't make her walk." Hoffman laughs. "I think we stopped traveling to contests together shortly after that."

Poppler seems to have harbored no grudge. In the February 2000 issue of *Surfing Girl* magazine, she observed: "Joyce is bigger than life in everything she does. She paved the way for all women to come."

In 1971, having carved a swath through history, Hoffman stopped surfing. She got married, had a daughter and retired from the sport for about ten years. "I had been so completely focused on surfing, I didn't know how to do it otherwise. It was either all or nothing."

Looking for something to replace surfing's physical challenge and adrenaline rush, she took up motorcycle racing. Then she switched to car racing. She pursued both with the intense devotion that she had given surfing. "I had quite a few wrecks, and then one in particular that made me realize that that was the last time I'd

Booming surf. Roaring engine. A pretty girl's smile. Triumph Spitfire Mk2.

Joyce Hoffman toured the world with Triumph as her sponsor. Courtesy Joyce Hoffman collection

have that type of wreck and walk away from it. So, I stopped racing."

Soon after, she and her husband divorced and Hoffman started managing the family properties, which include a horse ranch in San Juan Capistrano. In the early eighties, brother-in-law Fletcher lured her back to the surf with a new surfboard and the news that he had entered her in a contest. Off she went again. "I got into the whole longboard resurgence, got right back into the competition and ended up retiring again. Since then, I've

come back again and am now retired from competition for the third and final time. I surf a little more casually, and I try to keep my life in better perspective, but there's still a little voice in my head, like a broken record: 'You'd better get out there and practice or you're not going to be very good.'"

Hoffman's daughter, Samantha, turned the tables on her when she took up jumping horses at age twelve. "I couldn't stand watching her jump," says Hoffman. "I was a nervous wreck. I wouldn't have thought anything

Hoffman still rips today.
Photo: Jim Russi

about myself doing it. My mom had gotten used to watching her family do daredevil things. She takes her knitting with her and just knits faster when things get scary. So I told her, 'I can't handle this. You have to go with Samantha.' It turned out to be a nice thing, as my mom and daughter now have a wonderful relationship."

Two years ago, at age fifty, feeling that she needed a new challenge, Hoffman took to riding a six-four shortboard. "I do love it," she says. "I figure I have about one more year on that. Just being able to respond quickly enough and work that hard to push through the wave takes a lot out of me."

Hoffman pursues snowboarding with a familiar passion. "It's so much like surfing, only you never have to paddle out and it's always six foot and glassy," she says, flashing a big grin. "I wish it had been around when I was a kid. I like the powder, or a big bowl where I can do big, sweeping turns—like cut-backs on a wave."

Hoffman plans to surf for the rest of her life. "After taking that ten-year break, when I came back it felt like coming home. I didn't realize how much a part of my life surfing had become. I feel so rejuvenated by surfing. Nowadays, with the modern longboard, so many people of my era are getting back into the sport. It's not unusual to be surfing somewhere and have somebody paddle up to me and say, 'It's Joyce Hoffman, isn't it? I surfed with you, you won't remember me, but back in 1963 in Ocean Beach we surfed together!' It's such a wonderful connection, for both of us. It's not the ego thing; it's having shared an event that was so special to someone else and they feel comfortable enough to share it with you. If I hadn't gotten back into surfing, I wouldn't have that joy now."

Hoffman understands her place in history. "Marge Calhoun and her daughters really made surfing look possible for women and showed them that it was more than a sport. It's a mind-set, a lifestyle. Linda Benson pushed the sport. She was the first one to try to do it like the boys, with a more aggressive style. Then I took it and tried to do it exactly like the guys at that time. Margo Oberg came along and took it to the next level and opened the sport up to a lot of women through the longevity of her career. There have been other influential women along the way, but I think we set the pace and set the sport in motion. We advanced the sport in big leaps. Since then, the advances have been in small steps. That's just the luck of when we were born."

San Clemente, California, contest surfers: l to r, Joyce Hoffman, (unknown), Judy Dibble, Joey Hamasaki, Linda Benson, Margo Scotten. Photo: LeRoy Grannis

Making Waves

By Karin Moeller

In 1972, seventeen-year-old Mary Setterholm upset her mentor Jericho Poppler to win the U.S. Championships in Huntington Beach. Fortified by her success, she set off for Hawaii determined to prove her mettle on big waves and to organize women's competitions. She soon returned, disenchanted by the way the boy's-club industry viewed women's surfing, merely as an entertainment novelty and unworthy of serious attention.

In a November 1974 *Surfer* magazine article entitled "Equal Time," Setterholm echoed the frustrations of many women surfers of the time: "Why is surfing considered a man's sport, and why are women the minority in surfing? Well, there is a very dark side of surfing, and many people have been lost completely because of it. Surfing, which started out to be a cultural gathering of artists, has evolved into a state which reflects the paranoia, the prejudices and the hostilities of society as a whole." Eager to increase awareness of women's surfing—and elevate and legitimize its status within the industry—Setterholm and Poppler cofounded the Women's International Surfing Association (WISA) in 1975, with Setterholm as president.

The WISA sponsored pro/am events along the California coast. Its mission was to promote women's surfing, protect the ocean environment, encourage involvement through free instruction and espouse a healthy lifestyle. WISA's most successful contest was the Hang Ten Pro Invitational at Malibu, which helped boost media coverage and prize money for women. The first contest, in September 1975, drew contestants from both coasts plus Hawaii, Great Britain, Japan and Australia. Margo Godfrey Oberg captured first place and the $1,500 purse.

Before she had a chance to grow with WISA, the "dark side" of surfing Setterholm had written about showed its menacing face: she was sexually assaulted at a party by a group of surfers. "I came unglued and fled to New York City on a Greyhound bus," she says. "I'm sorry now that I left, but I didn't know how to stay."

In the years after the assault, Setterholm focused her boundless energy on being a New York City Fashion Institute of Technology student, wife, mother of five, physical trainer, wetsuit and clothing designer, triathlete and, back in California, retail store manager for Sport Chalet and Nordstrom. Her next goal was to become a lawyer, but in 1997, while cycling home from school at California State University at Dominguez Hills, adversity challenged her again. She was struck from behind by an automobile and rendered unconscious.

"My titanium bike was in pieces, there were two cracks in my helmet, but no bones were broken." Her injuries did, however, include brain swelling and some

Mary Lou Drummy shows her style.
Photo: LeRoy Grannis

54

amnesia. "I realize now it was the best thing that ever happened to me. God gave me a second chance. And the blessing was that I realized the grudges I was holding were speed bumps, slowing me down. I had a chip on my shoulder and it got knocked off."

Setterholm has made her peace with the past and returned to surfing. She applies much of her knowledge of physical training to surf instruction through her business, Surf Academy, in Manhattan Beach, California. "I see women needing to bond more," she says. "They need a group environment to help understand the culture of the sport. They also need upper body conditioning, which means more than just one or two lessons."

Setterholm is grateful to have found her home again at the beach. "I'm thankful for my hardships," she says. "I'm finally doing the work I was destined to do. The key to healing and success is acting. You can't be locked up in fear in life. It's like taking off on a wave—you can't think, 'Should I go or not?' If you do, it's gone."

After Setterholm left for New York City, Mary Lou Drummy took over as president of WISA. Poppler and Drummy remained involved in surfing through the seventies and eighties. Poppler continued to compete and then directed her energy to environmental activism, primarily through the Surfrider Foundation. Drummy stayed at the helm of the WISA for its lifespan—a total of seventeen years. The last WISA-sponsored contest was held in 1991. Drummy, who grew up surfing Malibu in the fifties, still

"gets in the water a couple days a week." She is devoted to promoting surfing to young people. For nearly fifteen years, she has coordinated approximately twenty pro/am surfing events a year—including women's specialty events—for the U.S. Surfing Federation (USSF), a California-based organization that qualifies surfers for U.S. amateur and world champion contests. "I believe strongly in these programs," she says. "I think surfing provides a good, social atmosphere and helps build self confidence. There's no other sport like it. You have no control over the conditions in which you surf. You have to know what you're doing and in the process of learning that, you learn a lot about yourself."

Drummy raised three sons and a daughter at the beach. All four surf and compete in amateur and pro/am contests. Drummy herself competed in pro/am events for twenty-five years, then stopped when she became involved in organizing events. "I loved competing, but not so much to win as to just stay in the water," she says. "I still have scars on my legs from surfing big, hairy waves at Huntington Beach pier."

When asked what has kept her involved in surfing for nearly fifty years, Drummy laughs and simply responds: "It's in my blood."

Mary Setterholm teaching at Surf Academy. Photo courtesy Mary Setterholm

Soul surfer. Photo: Jim Russi

Soul Surfer

After winning the Grand Masters division of the October 1999 Roxy Wahine Classic at San Onofre, Shelley Merrick wrote the following letter to contest producer Allan Seymour:

Shelley Merrick

In 1963, when I was seventeen, I entered a contest at Dockweiler Beach. It wasn't a point break, which I prefer, but I just went out and surfed and had a ball. I won the contest, and, as I was coming out of the water, Marge Calhoun walked out to meet me and told me what a beautiful surfer I was and to please remember to 'always remain a lady.' As this was how I was brought up by my family as well as by all the neighborhood boys, I never forgot her affirmation.

At fifty-four years of age, I had quietly decided that the San Onofre Roxy contest would be my 'swan song.' But I was so impressed with all those little girls and their warm enthusiasm that I want to be there for them and spend time with them. I want them to be great athletes and great young ladies. I want them to know that they can be great old ladies and still hang five while loving and caring for their children and families.

When they are career women in a board room filled with crisis or a parent guiding a thirteen-year-old, they can shut their eyes and momentarily 'grab the rail,' take a drop down a big face, or just keep pushing through a big set. It isn't all about surfing—it's about life and who you are and how you face every day.

Shelley Merrick grew up during the days of unspoiled and uncrowded California beaches and still appreciates the laid-back style of those years. Her home break was Latigo Cove, three miles north of Surfriders Beach at the famous surf spot, Malibu Point.

Merrick at Malibu, age 15.
Photo: Shelley Merrick collection

Her parents purchased their house in 1945, when there were only three in the cove. Merrick, her siblings and her friends enjoyed an idyllic lifestyle of swimming, riding horses on the beach and sailing with sheets and broom handles stuck in old surfboards.

Several of the families who eventually moved into the cove had experienced the twenties and thirties' era of surfing, and some were original members of the San Onofre Surf Club. One of them was "Uncle" John Larronde (now deceased) who had a quiver of old redwood surfboards made by a legendary, eccentric shaper named Bob Simmons. Larronde kept encouraging the young Merrick to go surfing. She was a competitive swimmer in school and had already taught herself to body surf and to ride surf mats, so the move to a surfboard was logical.

"When I was ten years old, Uncle John, Bruce Kemper and Matt Kivlin finally shoved me out on an old Simmons board," says Merrick. "I learned in what we called the Channel. Each time, I'd go a little further out. Nobody ever told me, 'This is what you do and how you do it.' I was a good swimmer, and I had good wave and water sense from bodysurfing and mat riding. Uncle John and the others would encourage me to paddle for waves.

"Of course, I became obsessed with surfing, and it became a lifestyle for me. I finally graduated from the redwood board to a nine-foot Joe Quigg balsa board belonging to Kemper. I'd go to my neighbor's house, knock on the door and ask to borrow the board. I'd have to drag it down to the beach to go surfing. I was lucky that our beach didn't get crowded until the late sixties."

Married in the seventies, when her three children reached ages eight, ten and twelve, Merrick and her family moved to Idaho for eight years. Divorce brought her back to the ocean in 1986. "I wanted my daughter and sons to be by the ocean. And I wanted them to truly understand rough water, so I enrolled them in junior lifeguard training. They all went on to be state lifeguards and also to teach junior lifeguard classes. They feel a oneness with the ocean, as I do. One of my greatest joys is to be out in the water and hear them yelling—'Mom, outside! There's a wave, go for it!'"

Merrick spent thirteen years as a single mom. Many of the ocean pursuits that she loved got set aside during this time. "You cannot go back and raise your children," she says, "but you can go back and surf and

Merrick having fun at Doheny, 1994.
Photo: Shelley Merrick collection

paddle. Once the kids were on their own, I started competing in paddling contests and in outrigger canoe events, in addition to surfing. I can still do all these things and my children are self-sufficient. For this, I feel a great satisfaction and I feel fortunate."

Merrick describes the impact of surfing on her life: "I think any sport teaches you discipline and decisiveness. I remember many years ago surfing the Ranch, and the surf just came up, like it does in Hawaii. And here I was in surf that had jumped from five feet to ten feet. I kept telling myself: 'Take a deep breath, don't get impulsive and stupid.' Surfing helps you learn to think on your feet—or on your board, if you will. You have to gather yourself and concentrate. The ocean is an ever-changing environment. You have to learn to adjust to it, because at any given moment something can happen to threaten your life. The choices you make as you maneuver through the surf and on the changing wave are a vehicle for survival, and for lifelong lessons."

Merrick competes because she is competitive by nature. In the sixties, she rode for surfboard manufacturer Dewey Weber. She surfed in many finals, and went head to head in the 1968 Huntington Beach Pro with Linda Benson, who won. "Marge Calhoun and I used to talk about how we were always at a disadvantage in contests. We both were tall, and we grew up surfing big point surf. In contests we'd often find ourselves in horrible, two-foot beach break. That's no excuse for not winning, but it made for a disadvantage.

"Competition is so different from free surfing," Merrick adds. "Competition is discipline. I have to think, 'I have fifteen minutes. I have to strategize, I have to think about what I'm doing.' I sometimes like being forced into that corner, because it pulls me up short a bit, and it takes some of that free-form spirit and channels it."

Merrick now surfs dawn patrol—the early hours before work—with fellow executives who find surfing at daybreak a truly soulful experience that carries them through the day no matter the pressures. She also surfs with longtime friends, Janet McPherson and Jackie Tanny, who, at fifty-seven, surfs every day (and is the daughter of commercial gym pioneer Vic Tanny). "My father [Judge John Merrick, Ret.] calls us 'the old gray gals of surfing,'" says Merrick. They are the epitome of the soul surfer, who surfs simply for the love of the sport.

Merrick is no stranger to the business world. She has held many management positions including tenure as a board member of the Surfrider Foundation, a nonprofit organization dedicated to preserving the ocean environment. She currently serves as executive director of the annual California Strawberry Festival in Oxnard.

"My life as it relates to the ocean is what keeps me going while I do the things I have to do," she says. "I take great pride in being a fifty-four-year-old mom of three and grandmother of one. I like being able to surf at dawn and then going to a board meeting in a gabardine suit—and nobody knowing the difference. I like that balance."

If she had to tip the scales one way? "I had to go to Universal Studios a few summers ago to do a bid on a project in which I was involved. I had on panty hose, a blazer and skirt—the whole outfit—and I also had my surfboard in the car because Leo—or Secos, as it was called in the sixties—was breaking. I drove by and it looked *so* good, I had to stop." She stripped off her professional clothes, pulled on her wetsuit, grabbed her board and started walking across the rocks, squinting into the afternoon sun and planning where to paddle out. "Here I am barefoot, wind blowing my board and throwing me off balance, and I think to myself, 'This is how I want people to see me."

Surfrider Foundation board members, l to r, Rell Sunn, Jericho Poppler, Mary McKay and Shelley Merrick, 1992. Photo: Shelley Merrick collection

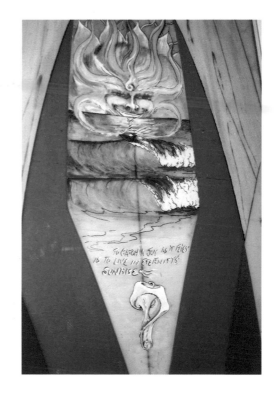

Above, design on ono of Merrick's
favorite old boards.
Photo: Andrea Gabbard
Other photos: Jim Russi

Danger Woman

by Karin Moeller

Californian Kim Hamrock says she was tagged with the nickname, "Danger Woman" by male surfers. "It was really hard when I started surfing twenty-something years ago. The guys in the water were hassling me and trying to discourage me from surfing—pushing me off waves and taking off in front of me. Although I didn't appreciate it at the time, it's made me what I am now."

Hamrock presumes that she earned her nickname because she likes to ride big waves and because she laughed at the guys who tried to intimidate her. "I grew up with three brothers who hassled me to no end," she says, "so when the guys in the water started teasing me it was nothing." She has continued to be in the vanguard of strong-minded, aware women surfers.

From the time she was six, Hamrock wanted to surf. "I saw the 1966 Surfing Championships contest on TV. I remember it was at the Huntington Beach pier, and the girls had helmets on and little vests with numbers. I thought, 'Oh, I gotta do that, that looks like the funnest thing in the world.'"

Unlike Linda Benson, Joyce Hoffman and Shelley Merrick, who grew up at surfing beaches, Hamrock lived twenty miles inland. She skateboarded and paddleboarded in a nearby lake and didn't start surfing consistently until age sixteen. "I think that's why to this day I'm such an animal, because I missed out," she says. "I don't think I'll ever ride enough waves to catch up."

Hamrock now runs Surf City Surfing Lessons in Huntington Beach. She feels that the level of women's surfing has been on the rise for the past five years. "When I grew up surfing, I surfed mostly Trestles, and I would see another girl out there maybe once or twice a year. Now there are so many girls out there, charging."

She sees the change as a general trend. "I think the shift hasn't come just in surfing. It's still a male-dominated sport, no doubt about it, but these girls don't even think about not getting into it just because men are doing it. Look at the jobs women are getting into nowadays. Think of other sports they're doing. Women aren't inhibited by the male/female thing that much, and it's just crossed over into surfing as well."

Hamrock predicts that the future of women's surfing lies in longboarding. "You can catch a lot more waves on a longboard," she explains. "It's hard to be more aggressive than men, since they have greater strength. And longboarding is more graceful than shortboarding. It's almost like dancing on your board, and therefore more conducive to women's surfing."

Hamrock has won four U.S. Surfing Championships, in both longboard and shortboard, as well as numerous West Coast championships. But the highlight of her career came in Puerto Escondido, Mexico, during the summer of '99 at the Central Surf First Annual Longboard Tube Riding Contest. "I've surfed the big waves on the North Shore of

Kim Hamrock, 1999.
Photo: Tomas Gibson

Oahu at least a dozen times," she says, "but this wave in Mexico was the most gnarly, scary, powerful wave I have ever encountered. I was the only woman invited to the contest. They asked ten of the male competitors if there should be a woman invited and, if so, who? And eight of them said 'Kim,' and two of them said 'None.'

"So I did it! I went out there and I held my own. The men surfed it; I felt like I just survived it. It was a great time for it to happen for me, because I thought at forty I was getting too old for the big stuff, but it just sparked my fire. Now I figure for at least another ten years I'm going to be charging the biggest waves that I possibly can."

Hamrock is called "Danger Woman" because of her love of big waves. Puerto Escondido.
Photo: Jim Russi

Sunn heading out to her favorite break.
Photo: Jim Russi

Heart of the Sea

When Rell Sunn's grandmother gave her the middle name of Kapolioka'ehukai, Heart of the Sea, she must have sensed destiny.

Rell Sunn

Sunn began surfing at four, guided into the waves by her "uncle," the great surfer Buffalo Keaulana, who also taught her to dive and spear. Sunn and her four siblings grew up on the beach near Makaha point, fighting over the one surfboard they shared between them. "If you lost out, you'd grab one off the beach and surf as long as you could before the owner found out," Sunn playfully recalled during an interview in 1995. "As I got a little older, every board I ever got spent a night in my room, sometimes in the bed. I'd touch the rails and fondle it. Can you imagine being four and knowing what love is?"

Sunn's love affair with surfing connected her to the ocean environment. She could predict the wind, the waves and the tides. Throughout her life, as she received inspiration and sustenance from the elements, so she gave back to all she met, to all with whom she shared a wave or a cup of coffee, in the Hawaiian spirit of Aloha. When she passed away in January 1998 at age forty-seven, after a fifteen-year battle with metastasized breast cancer, the sudden silence of her heartbeat stunned and saddened her fellow Hawaiians as well as a worldwide community of surfers.

Sunn's skills and accomplishments were numerous. She surfed with style, feminine grace and typical Hawaiian humor—sometimes sitting in a lawn chair atop her surfboard, other times with her dog Shane perched on the nose of her board. She once said, "Dogs go out to surf once, and from that point on, they know they're special."

A trip to California in 1966 with Duke Kahanamoku to attend a world championship sparked Sunn's love of travel. She went on to surf around the globe, both in competition as one of the founders of the women's pro circuit and as a promoter of surfing among youth. She was an all-around waterwoman, paddling outrigger canoes, free diving and spearfishing. She was Hawaii's first full-time female lifeguard, an honor in a culture where proficiency in the water is widely respected. She hosted a radio program and wrote newspaper and magazine articles. She taught hula with the same devotion and sense of importance with which she taught water safety. She ushered hundreds of young boys and

The Queen of Makaha. Photo: Jim Russi

girls into surfing through her annual Menehune Contest, which celebrated its silver anniversary in November 1999 and continues today through the guidance of her daughter, Jan. Sunn arranged sponsorship for and chaperoned two dozen Menehune surfers to the Biarritz Surf Festival in France. She served on the board of the Surfrider Foundation, an organization devoted to preserving the ocean environment. Like Kahanamoku, Sunn served as Hawaii's surfing ambassador for more than thirty years.

When Sunn's friends speak of her, they speak of joy, humor and generosity. They speak of optimism in the face of the insidious disease that stalked the last third of her life. Sunn's husband, surfer and writer Dave Parmenter, speaks of her courage and selflessness: "When the demons of fear came to her, she picked up the phone and called someone else and made them laugh and brightened their day. She never wept or felt pity. She was unvanquished."

Momi Keaulana, wife of Buffalo and mother of surf stars Brian and Rusty, adds: "Rell would help anybody. If she had something you wanted, she'd give it to you."

Keaulana especially appreciated Sunn's playful nature: "On her radio program, she gave the surf forecast for Makaha. A couple of times, when the surf was flat, she said the waves were really rolling, and they were six feet *deep*. I asked her, 'Were you lonesome that day?' She said, 'Exactly!'"

Sunn's spirit and generosity touched younger generations of surfers. Twenty-two-year-old Megan Abubo captured fourth place in the Roxy Pro at Sunset Beach in December 1999, putting her in the top echelon of the women's circuit. As a youngster, she had competed in Sunn's Menehune Contest. "I first met Rell when I was ten," Abubo recalls. "She gave me some of the best advice I've ever heard from anyone. Her attitude, her outlook on life, her respect for the ocean, should be spread throughout the world."

Kathy Terada met Sunn in 1978 in hula class, and the two became close friends. "I was twenty-six; she was my hula sister. She was so full of life and joy. She could remember the details of stories and retell them over and over, and they were always funny.

Top: Rell Sunn, Makaha. Photo: Jim Russi

Bottom: Buffalo, Momi, Brian and Chad Keanu Keaulana at the 1999 Menehune Contest, Makaha, 1999. Photo: Andrea Gabbard

I'd surf with Rell, but she was so much better I preferred to watch her. She could do anything in the water. We'd surf early in the morning—dawn patrol—and afterwards have chocolate donuts. I met my husband at Makaha. When we got married, we held the ceremony at Makaha and Rell provided the chocolate donuts."

Margo Oberg first called Sunn the Queen of Makaha. Although there was a hint of royalty in Sunn's appearance and bearing, she was extremely accessible and popular, often in spite of herself. Longtime surf photographer Warren Bolster explains: "She could paddle a canoe, dive as well as any guy, surf big waves. I was always a little frustrated she didn't do more for her own benefit. I mean, she didn't do anything to promote herself. You had to draw it out of her."

It was only fitting that the Queen of Makaha be given a royal burial. Brian Keaulana coordinated the ceremony. The offering, said Keaulana, was to be "surf, sand and sound. Bring sand from your beaches, water from your surf and a conch shell for the sound of a thousand blowing at once," just as it was more than a century ago when Hawaii's Queen Emma was put to rest.

More than three thousand mourners—or celebrants of life, as Momi called them—showed up for the ceremony. Parmenter carried her ashes in a light green glass bowl (recalling Sunn's own words: "I often think of myself as a gypsy glass ball, floating from one shore to another in perfect surf, fragile, yet arriving and departing in one piece."). After the eulogy, Parmenter, Keaulana, Rell's daughter Jan and her brother Eric paddled out to the empty waves of Makaha in Rell's canoe, *Kapolioka'ehukai*. They paddled to the blow hole, Sunn's favorite lineup spot at Makaha. A mournful note echoed from

Sunn made the hula shine.
Photo: Jeff Divine

the conch shells blowing on shore.

Momi shares a story that most certainly will become a Hawaiian legend: "We asked Kaneloa, the Hawaiian God of the Sea, to please take Rell's ashes and hold her to his bosom. When Dave threw Rell's ashes into the blow hole, it suddenly swirled up and sucked them all right down. Everyone on the beach started crying. I said to them, 'Make a joyful sound. Rell is where she wants to be, in God's hands. A spirit has been born.'"

Momi continues to promote that attitude. "People elaborate on Rell's death. I call it a celebration of life. People came from all over the world and so many were sad. Everybody had a different Rell to deal with. Mine was very simple. She loved life, she loved surfing and she loved people. Now, every year at the Menehune Contest, we all say, 'Thank you, Auntie Rell, for the waves!'"

Sunn is considered one of the best longboarders, ever.
Photo: Jeff Divine

The Spirit of Rell

By Robin "Zeuf" Janiszeufski

Surfing removes the need to close my eyes and seek the voice inside. The face of the wave defines my being. I hear, see, smell and taste the ocean. Through surfing, I experience a pure joy and higher-mindedness that has no substitute. Surfing has become the metaphor for how I move through life on land.

This has not always been the case. In January 1993, I was flying to the Islands for a second visit, this time to surf. The trip had been an inspiration of a friend traveling with me. We planned to meet with her family and friends upon our arrival in Maui.

I had taken up longboarding after years of being a bodysurfer in Northern California's refreshing but often brutally cold ocean. I was so excited to be in the warm waters of Hawaii, wearing only a bathing suit, that I could hardly stay in my seat.

I passed the time on the long flight by reading a surfing magazine. On the cover was a photo of Hawaiian surfer Rell Sunn. I had heard so much about her already, and this particular article was very inspirational. I was captivated. Her beauty, grace and power embodied surfing. Her spirit and tenacity in fighting breast cancer awed me. Sunn had undergone a mastectomy in 1982. But the breast cancer subsequently had metastasized and was declared terminal. For ten years, she underwent clinical trials and kept the dire prognosis unrealized. As a nurse, I admire how certain people, when faced with potential life-threatening diseases, often find an inner source of healing. Rell Sunn seemed to have found that source.

After reading the article, I closed my eyes and thought, "How I wish I could meet this woman, or at least watch her surf." When the plane landed in Hawaii, Rell's image stayed in the forefront of my mind as I walked into the warm Maui sunshine. She lived on Oahu, in Makaha, so the chances of meeting her were slim. Still, I thought, perhaps, someday . . .

I had just settled in at the house we were renting when a knock at the door signaled someone's arrival—it was a beautiful Hawaiian woman and one of the owners of the house. She introduced herself as Nell and greeted me warmly. Then she called to someone coming in from the garage. In walked Kula, as striking as her sister Nell. She, too, greeted me warmly and said, "Hey Zeuf, we hear you like to surf, so we're taking you out today. Sorry we're late, but we had to pick up our sister from the airport. She's visiting us here in Maui."

In the Hawaiian spirit of Aloha—the giving of love and friendship and feeling it come back—both Nell and Kula had brought food, which already was being opened and passed around. Then came more laughter, and yet another woman entered the house. As I turned to say hello, I almost dropped the sushi Kula had prepared. Rell Sunn was standing in front of me.

After more hugs and greetings all around, Nell and Rell started in on one of their trademark hysterical stories. It was all I could do to maintain my *haole* composure as not just one but three Sunn siblings walked into my life. My world was changed forever by that meeting.

Nell, Kula and Rell were determined to take me surfing and teach me what they knew—and what I could handle. This was done with great enthusiasm, hooting and hollering. By the time we went surfing our circle had grown to include other family and friends from the area. Each of us yelled encouragement to the other. We were quite the group, sharing great fun, great rides and, for some of us, great wipeouts!

My daytime adventures with the Sunn sisters were incredible. We surfed, ate good food, went flea-marketing, surfed some more, shopped antique stores, ate again, laughed, acted silly, watched the sun set and discussed life. Evenings evolved into poignant talks with Rell about surfing, diving, paddling, relationships and, in particular, breast cancer. Her openness and willingness to share her feelings were gifts she bestowed upon me.

When Rell spoke of Makaha, her home, she would speak of beauty. She talked of people whom she loved, of spear fishing and of surfing the most recent waves that graced the beach near her house. Yes, Rell had cancer,

but cancer certainly didn't have her. I came to realize that Rell's daily healing was only peripherally related to Western medicine. The wellspring of her life energy began at a cellular level, buoyed by Hawaiian ocean swells and saltwater. These elements were her true medicine.

I also discovered that the Sunn sisters' humor is unmatched, their stories and activities nonstop. Their world was one of waves, laughter, joy and hope. This world spilled over into mine as they opened up their hearts and took me in as family. As I reluctantly prepared to return home, we discussed plans for my next trip.

All too soon I was back in Northern California's cold water, wearing a wetsuit once again. One day, while changing into my clothes after surfing, I noticed a lump on the surface of my breast. I shrugged it off as a swollen lymph node from a recent sore throat. Several weeks later, however, the lump had not gone down. I wanted to ignore it, but from my training as a nurse I knew I could not. I was eventually diagnosed with breast cancer, just two and a half months after meeting the Sunn sisters.

I decided that now was the time to practice all the joy and healing power that I recently had been shown. I notified the sisters. Our phone calls during the next sev-

Sunn and Zeuf, Sunset Beach.
Photo: Robin Janiszeufski

eral months were frequent; we discussed the prognosis and treatment options at length. They made me promise to come over for recovery time, after surgery. Their humor helped me laugh through my tears.

They also encouraged me to get back in the water as soon as I could. Surfing became my therapy, my life beyond traditional Western medical treatment. My family and friends in California were stunned at my rapid recovery and buoyant attitude. My doctors advised me to slow down, but I could not. I headed for the waves as soon as I could use my arm to paddle, and my physical strength would hold out long enough to catch a few waves. Rell

had shown me how not to let cancer get in the way of living.

My world changed when I met the Sunn sisters. I knew it would be changed again by breast cancer. I learned to close my eyes and listen so that I could heal on a cellular level. When I surfed, I opened my eyes and heeded the call to a higher level of being.

Several years have passed. I have visited the Sunn sisters many times. I have met the rest of the family, including Rell's parents, Elbert and Roan, Rell's daughter Jan, and her older sister Val (who shares the family attributes of beauty and grace), brother Eric and their extended family. Their generosity is limitless. I am a better person for knowing them.

In 1998, when Rell passed over, she left behind a gift of unequalled spirit. The magical spell of her presence remains with me, as with all who knew her. I thank Rell for the beautiful waves I have seen and ridden since and for the perspective that surfing provides.

Zeuf at her home break of Santa Cruz.
Photo: Elizabeth Pepin

The Longest Ride

In 1966, at age thirteen, Margo Godfrey was ranked fourth in the world among women surfers. Her professional career went on to span more than three decades. She won the World Championship in 1968, 1977, 1980 and 1981 as well as numerous amateur and pro contests. Her last pro contest was in 1992; she placed fourth. Hers is the longest women's surfing career on record.

Margo Oberg

She was coached early in her career by former World Champion Mike Doyle, who also shaped her surfboards. Doyle says he recognized Godfrey's talent the first time he saw her surf at La Jolla Shores. "I said to myself, 'There's the future women's champion.' Margo was the first girl to actually carve turns and link them together. She had a stand-up-straight style and dropped low in her stance when she was about to execute a turn or cut-back. She rode like a guy and was the first in my mind to be better than most of the guys. She was also brave, whether it was twelve-foot Sunset or trying a macrobiotic diet. She would give it a go and see what happened."

Godfrey's bravado in surfing did not carry over completely to her personal life. She wrestled with her competitive desire to win every contest she entered and her desire to be liked by her peers. After stunning the surfing community by winning the world title at age fifteen in 1968, Godfrey came in second to Sharon Weber in the 1970 world contest held in Australia. "I had to go back to Santa Barbara High School and live through the eleventh and twelfth grades not being world champion. People kept asking, 'What happened, why didn't you win?' The loss was so devastating that I retired."

She moved to Kauai in 1971, at age eighteen. The following year, she married Steve Oberg. She was coaxed out of retirement in 1974 to compete in a Malibu contest against Mary Lou Drummy and Jericho Poppler. After winning there, Oberg agreed to compete with six other women in the men's Smirnoff contest in 1975. Contest organizer Fred Hemmings placed one woman in each men's heat. Oberg won third place overall, and first in the women's, for a prize of a thousand dollars. She continued to compete. Whenever she didn't win, she was deeply disappointed in herself.

Oberg opened a surf school on Kauai in 1977, then dove into the 1978 season neck and neck with Lynne Boyer. Oberg and Boyer battled over first and second ranking all year long. At the end of the year, in the preliminary heat of the deciding contest at

Teenage Margo Godfrey—in a pretty party dress—at an award ceremony.
Photo: LeRoy Grannis

Opposite: Oberg, Sunset Beach, Hawaii.
Photo: Jeff Divine

Sunset Beach, Oberg's leash broke. "I spent the entire heat swimming for my board. Lynne won and I ended up second."

Characteristically, Oberg went into a slump and refused to compete in 1979, the year that Boyer again won the title. Instead, Oberg signed on as a commentator for ABC. "Don't you love how I lose?" she reflects today. "I quit and pout for a while." She returned to the tour and won world titles in 1980 and 1981.

Oberg competed for the World Cup in 1982 while nursing her first son, Shane. When her second son Jason was born in 1987, Oberg was still competing and still trying to make friends. "I was really sensitive. I wanted this big camaraderie, but I also wanted to win. When you win, people find fault. They say, 'Oh, she just wins because she's a wave hog,' or 'She's too aggressive.' I used to think, 'How can I win if I'm not aggressive?'"

Oberg felt isolated by this criticism. "The cruel part is that everyone was nice to my face, and then I'd hear things from other people about the negative comments they made about me behind my back. I could read the waves and paddle hard, so I caught a lot of waves—and a lot of flak. The backstabbing thing made for a really lonely time. Steve and I were Pentecostal, so when he traveled with me, we'd seek out a church for fellowship. I didn't care about the doctrine that much—I liked the fellowship."

Husband Steve coached her, helped her map out a strategy and kept her focused on it. "He also kept me away from the other competitors. He'd say, 'You want everyone to like you, and you end up giving away waves.' I did that in the last pro contest I entered, in '92. I was in the final, in a heat with Wendy Botha. This perfect wave came through and we were both in position for it. If she caught it and made it, she would win the world title. I thought, should I hassle her for that wave? I didn't have enough points to win the title. So, I just paddled into the channel. She caught it and won. I knew I could never enter another contest again because I no longer cared if I won. Before, I had a real hunger for everyone to say I was the best. Then I realized I didn't care anymore."

She admits that today it's hard to just

World Champion Oberg and her sponsor car.
Photo: Jeff Divine

1967 contestants Joyce Hoffman, Mimi Munro, Margo
Oberg and Joey Hamasaki. Photo: LeRoy Grannis

watch a contest simply for the joy of it. "I start worrying if I still fit in. Then another part of me knows I could go out there and surf those ten-foot waves as well as the pros do now. The rowdy in me wants to go dancing; the other side wants to go to church!"

Oberg still runs her surf school on Kauai. She has taught and inspired an entire generation of surfers who speak of her in glowing terms. Both Rochelle Ballard, who has competed on the pro tour for nine years, and longboard competitor Koral McCarthy grew up in Kauai and benefited from Oberg's influence.

"Margo was definitely inspirational and steered me in a direction that I thought was feasible as a pro," says Ballard. "When I got into big-wave surfing in my senior year of high school, I started surfing with her more. It was pretty cool, just hanging out with her and learning how to ride big waves."

As youngsters, McCarthy and her sister Melanie used to sit in the inside bowl at Hanalei Bay and watch as "this woman paddled out to the point and caught all the good waves. We didn't know at the time who she was, but she sure could surf! Then in our teens we started doing contests and realized who Margo is. She always has been an inspiration to us and has encouraged us. I can only imagine all the changes that Margo has seen in women's surfing."

One of the biggest changes was the transition from longboards to shortboards in the late sixties. In general, longboards are nine feet or longer, and shortboards are seven feet or shorter. Boards between seven and nine feet long are called "funboards" and offer the stability of the longboard and some of the maneuverability of

a shortboard. Oberg started competing on longboards in 1964. "I really liked nose riding and still do," she says. "I was small—only weighed about a hundred pounds. It wasn't hard for me to make the transition to shortboards, because I always had really light longboards, designed for my weight. Right before the 1968 world championship contest, I switched to a shortboard. It was so much easier and quicker to turn and cut back."

Although the transition from surf pro to surf legend did not come as easily, Oberg says she has no regrets. When asked to name her all-time favorite surfer, she says, "Probably me," and laughs. "As a young girl, I would tell

Top: Oberg (left) and Boyer (right) at an Op Pro contest. Photo: Jeff Divine

Bottom: Oberg in Puerto Rico. Photo: LeRoy Grannis

myself, 'I'm going to surf until I'm sixteen, then I'll be a regular girl.' I used to run around in T-shirts and wetsuits, with wet hair all the time. I kept looking forward to the day when I would be sixteen and able to wear pretty party dresses and hang out with cute guys. I was going to be a normal girl. But it never happened, and now I'm glad about it."

When asked to name her favorite break, she rattles off several names as though flipping through a Rolodex of famous surf spots, then stops: "Sunset Beach. I felt that Sunset Beach was the master. I never even got close to what I really wanted to do on a Sunset wave. I just dropped in and turned, barely holding on. It was my favorite because it was scary and I never got sick of it. Today, since I teach so much, I like friendly little waves. I'm really not into turning any more. I just stand there and ride the wave. Older surfers will understand what I'm saying."

She adds, "In contests, I knew I had to take more chances. To be a competitor, you have to be willing to show off a bit. And to be a standout, you have to rip."

And she did.

Oberg shows her distinct surfing style.
Photographer unknown; courtesy Roxy collection

How Contests Are Judged

In competitive surfing, there is no finish line, no stationary goal, no set course. The playing field is one of change, surprise and sometimes disappointment. Wave size, type and frequency are not guaranteed, of course, unlike conditions in a sport like basketball. Success depends on scoring high points on a certain number of waves during a set period of time. Because of this, as four-time world champion Lisa Andersen says, "Wave selection becomes a crucial tactic."

A contest consists of a series of elimination heats in which there are two or four surfers in each heat leading to the final. The competitors wear different colored jerseys to help the judges identify them. About ten minutes before their heat begins, contestants can enter the water to paddle out near the designated competition area, where they wait for a horn to sound the beginning of the heat. Then they have a limited period of time to catch and ride waves while judges on shore rate their performance. The time frame averages half an hour, and the best four of ten waves caught and ridden are judged. The time can be longer or shorter and the number of waves also can vary, depending upon surf conditions or the type of contest. For example, if the surf is inconsistent and there are not enough waves rolling in to allow each contestant a fair chance of catching enough waves, the time might be extended. Youngsters in amateur contests often compete in shorter time frames and on fewer waves.

Sound simple and totally fair? It's not. In fact, the objectivity of surf contest judging has been debated hotly, to say the least, ever since somebody proposed the idea of crowning a champion.

In the seventies, judges used a system that tallied points per maneuver and multiplied them by a "wave size factor" determined by the head judge. This complicated and ultimately subjective system was dropped, and a pure point-scoring function was assigned to judges.

In 1982, when the Association of Surfing Professionals (ASP) was formed by a contingent of surfers, these methods were thrown out in favor of others that emphasized good surfing and minimized subjectivity. The current ASP judging criteria, which were revised early in 2000, declare: "The surfer must perform committed radical maneuvers in the most critical sections of a wave with style, power and speed to maximize scoring potential. Innovative and progressive surfing will be taken into account when rewarding points for committed surfing. The surfer who executes these criteria with the highest degree of difficulty and control on the better waves shall be rewarded with the highest scores."

A point-scoring system is still used, from zero (bad) to ten (excellent). The panel of five judges (three international and two local) is controlled and directed by the ASP head judge. Final scores are determined by dropping the scores of the highest-scoring and lowest-scoring judges, and averaging the scores of the remaining three.

To explain key phrases in the criteria: "Committed radical maneuvers" include reentries, cut-backs, floaters, aerials and tube rides. How extreme they are, followed by the amount of control and commitment put into each, determines the score. If a surfer only completes 90 percent of a maneuver and then falls off her board, no score is given. This frustrates some surfers, who feel that this rule forces them to surf more conservatively in contests than they would in free surfing.

The "critical section of a wave" is the pocket or the closest position to the breaking curl of the wave, also known as the take off position. Exceptions to this critical section are bowl sections at, for example, Sunset Beach in Hawaii, Bell's Beach in Australia and St. Leu on Reunion Island in the Indian Ocean.

"Better waves" refers to wave selection, the most important factor in a surfer's heat. The wave selected dictates the types of maneuvers performed. Therefore, the best waves may not always be the biggest.

In tandem surfing, the focus of the judging criteria shifts from maneuvers performed by the surfer on the wave to maneuvers performed by the man and woman on the surfboard. In most contests, participants are required to perform up to four maneuvers during a heat—such as the Cradle, Swan, Grass Shack, Arabesque—and are judged on their form and success in completing the maneuver.

Judge's stand at San Onofre.
Photo: Karin Moeller

If a surfer hinders another surfer during a contest, interference will be called whether or not scoring loss results. Points can be lost or the offending surfer disqualified, depending on the severity of the interference. A common offense is "dropping in." This occurs when the offender takes off on a wave in front of a surfer who is taking off in the pocket. Another common offense happens after a surfer catches a wave and then intentionally paddles back out in the middle of the lineup and prevents another surfer from either catching or riding a wave. (When paddling back out to the lineup, one should head to either side of the break.) In noncompetitive or "free" surfing, avoiding these offenses is common etiquette.

Contest organizers attempt to schedule competitions in places and at times of the year when waves are known to break. Most notable are March and April in Australia, May in Tahiti, May through August in the U.S., June in South Africa, August in France, September in Spain, October in Japan, and October through December in Hawaii. A waiting period of several days to a week or longer is declared, to allow the best possible surf conditions. Lack of waves or bad weather can force postponement or cancellation of a day's events. As an example, the start of the 1999 Roxy Pro at Sunset Beach was postponed a week, waiting for suitable waves. Friday, December 3 proved to be worth the wait, delivering nearly perfect six-to-ten foot waves for the contest. The following day, the men's contest had to be postponed in the face of dangerously high surf.

Ultimately, the ocean has the last vote.

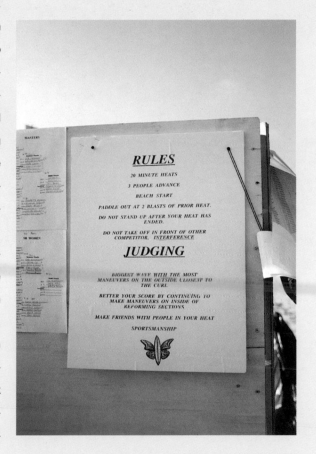

Judging guidelines, Roxy Wahine Classic, San Onofre, 1999. Photo: Andrea Gabbard

Surfing as Art

The desire to be number one, to be world champion, was like a burning fire in Lynne Boyer. "Surfing was my life," she says. "I ate, drank, breathed and slept surfing. I dreamed of being like Martina Navratilova, having all these sponsors, being in magazines everywhere, signing autographs.

"What the pros are doing today is what we worked so hard for. I get a little envious, but I'm happy to see all the women out there ripping—finally!"

Boyer first surfed as a child at the beach by her family's summer house in Wildwood, New Jersey, on rubber mats and Styrofoam boards. One day, her father, then an Army doctor, announced that he was going to be transferred to Colorado or Hawaii. Boyer was elated. "I thought, 'If we move to Hawaii, I'm going to surf. If Colorado, I'll ski.'"

Luckily for women's surfing, the destination was Hawaii. In November 1968, when Boyer was eleven, the family moved to Oahu. Upon his discharge from the Army, Boyer's father started the cancer clinic at Queens Medical Center in Honolulu. He also found time to take his daughter surfing. "He didn't surf that much himself, but he liked going to the beach," says Boyer. "He first got me out on a nine-foot-six tanker foam board at Pokai Bay. Sometimes, he'd pick me up from school on Wednesdays, and we'd go out surfing in the afternoons."

Boyer instantly loved the feeling of surfing. "One of my earliest memories is of being on that first board, standing up. I remember the speed and the clatter of the water hitting the underside of the board, how it all sounded and felt. The rush, the exhilaration, the speed. I was stoked from that point on."

She quickly graduated to a smaller, lighter surfboard and, throughout her teens, competed in amateur contests through the Hawaii Surfing Association (HSA). She did not hesitate in becoming a professional—although she did falter at first before some waves. "I was part of the first women's tour in 1976. I remember I was scared at our first event, the Smirnoff Pro in Hawaii, because I hated big waves then. Before that, I had made this commitment to catch the biggest wave I could ever catch. I went out in a huge swell at Makaha and almost drowned with that commitment. I got caught inside under three waves in a row, in

Boyer and Rell Sunn, waiting for their heat.
Photo: Jeff Divine

fifteen-foot point surf. After the third wave, I saw black I had been held under so long. By the time I got out of danger, I was seeing stars, and that scared me away from going back out in big waves."

Boyer laughs. "With the lure of celebrity and money, it wasn't that hard to get me out there again. I surfed at Sunset Beach, surfed through my fear, and started riding big waves again. The Makaha experience taught me to be careful and cautious, and to be in really good shape."

Yet Boyer did not try to mimic the methods of her nemesis, Margo Oberg. "She was strong and her turns were smooth. She could catch and ride bigger waves with a smoother style than most of us. I was more radical, more contemporary in style. Margo was more traditional."

Oberg agrees with this assessment, and adds: "Lynne came on the scene and got the full fanfare because she surfs, she's an artist, she's very pretty. She didn't talk much. But technically, you could say she was more radical. She had wild red hair, she would paint her boards all up, she *looked* radical."

Boyer first met Oberg at the Smirnoff contest in 1975. She describes her rivalry with Oberg as similar to that between world champion tennis players, Martina Navratilova and Chris Evert.

Boyer jokes about their rivalry. "Today, we laugh about it, but back then we wouldn't give each other an edge, no way. I was shy and kept everything inside, which made the tour kind of hard for me. My secret weapon, though, was my knowledge of the wave. At Sunset, Margo and I forced each other into the pit, behind the peak, to take off. The other women were in the channel. Margo and I were the only two behind the peak, catching the wave in the really prime spot.

"Later, I saw that [Aussie pro] Jodie Cooper had the same sort of guts in big waves. Most women today don't get the opportunity to surf big waves in contests. So many of the events are held in places where the surf is inconsistent."

She continues: "It's good that Layne Beachley (world champion in 1998 and 1999) has Ken Bradshaw coaching her. Ken was my mentor at Sunset Beach. He knew that lineup and taught it to me. That's so important in big surf, because there is so much current pulling you off the mark. You have to have points of orientation—some landmark on the beach, or boils in the water. Otherwise, you can get caught in the wrong place and get hurt."

Both Boyer and Oberg trained in big waves. "We made sure we had the right equipment and stayed in shape," says Boyer. "That's one of the highest feelings ever, riding a huge wave. You just feel on top of the world when you're done. There aren't too many feelings like that now in my life. It's a hard adjustment, coming down off that."

At forty-four, Boyer is slender and fit and still has her trademark wild red hair. She also

A winner's smile.
Photo: Jeff Divine

retains a trace of shyness but laughs easily. While she surfs regularly, her prime focus is on her blossoming career as an artist. Her paintings reflect the domain she loves—the sea, the life forms in and around it, waves. She has also painted surfing self-portraits. To pay the bills, she cleans houses. When asked if this is what a two-time world champion (she won the crown in 1978 and 1979) expected to be doing after her surfing career, Boyer shrugs and grins. "Sometimes it's a frustration, but mostly because I like to have at least a solid week to paint. I get something going, then I have to stop and go clean a house."

Boyer stopped following the tour in the early eighties but surfed events in Hawaii until 1987. After that, Boyer says she lost the desire to compete. "I have no regrets. I had so much fun surfing as a pro. I'm so grateful I got to do that and be among the first women pros."

The ocean is the wellspring of Boyer's creativity. "I get a lot of joy from the ocean, from being out there in it, with nature, the waves and the freedom that I feel when I'm out there. I get the same feelings when I paint."

Future plans include a possible move to the mainland with her partner, Reka, a physical oceanographer. "My goal is to become a successful artist, make a living off of it and not have to clean houses," she says. "Surfing came easy. Art is not so easy. I prefer to live by the ocean, but I am willing to try a new territory."

Boyer laughs and tosses her hair; she has conquered new territory before. "It's all part of the dues you pay to be an artist."

Boyer says her "secret weapon" was her
knowledge of the wave. Photo: Jeff Divine

The Pioneers of Women's Pro Surfing

The seventies were "The Dark Ages of Surfing," says former pro surfer Jericho Poppler, 1970 U.S. Women's Champion and 1976 World Champion. "It was during the height of Vietnam and the resulting social unrest in this country affected the surfing community," she says. "Amateur surfing was in the doldrums from 1973 to 1976. The men had gone pro and the women were almost totally neglected."

In 1976, a women's tour was developed by Fred Hemmings' newly formed International Professional Surfing (IPS), an organization that governed the international pro circuit. After auspicious beginnings, the women's tour limped along for several years, often staging just four or five pro events per year.

In 1979, Poppler spearheaded the formation of the Women's Pro Surfing (WPS) association. WPS membership was composed of pro women on the tour, including Poppler, Lynne Boyer, Margo Oberg, Rell Sunn, Cherie Gross, Linda Davoli, Debbie Melville Beacham, Becky Benson, Liz Benevidez and Brenda Scott (who later founded the wetsuit company Hotline). The WPS intended to unite pro women in one voice to address their needs and provide a vehicle for presenting recommendations and proposals to event directors. Poppler became an outspoken proponent of increased media coverage and prize money, a campaign that often angered and alienated the men's surfing establishment—especially in Australia, where sponsorship dollars for women began to fizzle and some contests were canceled.

From the mid-seventies to the mid-eighties, the women's tour was plagued by slim purses, poor surf conditions and humiliating distractions. In one Australian contest, for example, the first-place woman took home $1,500, the man, $35,000. In most contests, the best surf was reserved for the men's event. Often, while women were out competing in their final surfing heats, all eyes in the crowd—and of the media—were focused on the women competing in the bikini contest on the beach. Some pro women joked halfheartedly that it would be more profitable to win the bikini contest and receive a lucrative modeling contract and an all-expenses-paid trip to Hawaii.

Debbie Beacham, 1982 World Champion.
Photo: Debbie Beacham collection

The clout of the WPS had begun to wane under this intense chauvinism when, in 1981, the year before she won the World Championship, Debbie Beacham resurrected the organization in an effort to rebuild the sponsorship base for the women's tour. Beacham secured several non-surf sponsors, including Michelob, Mazda, Bucci Sunglasses and The Limited. To increase visibility, says Beacham, "we did a lot of our own marketing. We also organized our own pro/am events, such as a 'triathlon' of Hobie Cat catamaran racing, sailboarding and surfing, to generate more interest."

In 1982, the Association of Surfing Professionals (ASP) was formed and in 1983 took over the men's and women's tour from the IPS. ASP founder Ian Cairns invited the women's tour to join the ASP. Cairns promised to try to get women better prize money and sponsors. Realizing that the chances were slim that the WPS could garner a sponsorship base large enough to run its own tour, the women agreed to join, even though, as Beacham states, "surfing was still the most ego-driven, male-dominated sport on the planet."

The women's tour remains under the sanction of the ASP, but women are working towards developing separate, women-only events. Pros Rochelle Ballard, Megan Abubo, Kate Skarrat, Prue Jeffries and Layne Beachley are picking up where Poppler and Beacham left off. They

Jericho Poppler performing on her signature
board. Photo: Jeff Divine

have their work cut out for them. The total prize money for the men's 2000 World Championship Tour is $2.1 million; for women, it is just under $500,000. In 2001, the women's tour venues will undergo an overhaul. An increase in total prize money also is expected as the popularity of women's surfing increases and boosts the economic base.

Both Poppler and Beacham have remained active in surfing. Poppler became an environmental activist in 1984 as a charter member of the Surfrider Foundation, a non-profit organization founded in 1984 to preserve the ocean environment. She served on the board for five years and is still active in her local chapter in Southern California. She drafted several women surfers onto the board in the eighties, including Rell Sunn, Karen McKay and Shelley Merrick. In 1992, Poppler started Jericho's Kids for Clean Waves, a surfing contest for kids age sixteen and younger that includes educational and outreach programs. "We do beach cleanups and have a different theme, a different beach, every year," says Poppler. "The money we get from entry fees for the event goes to that year's project." The contest attracts more than two hundred kids each year.

Poppler has a vested interest in keeping the ocean clean and healthy. Her five children, ranging in age from one to fifteen, are surfers, divers and swimmers—beach kids in her tradition. Her physician husband, Greg Bartlow, doesn't surf. "He loves living near the ocean," Poppler explains, adding, "Surfing is a lifestyle that we want to preserve for our kids." These days, when she's not hauling kids to school or engaged in other activities, Poppler often can be found riding her Jericho model surfboard, shaped by *Endless Summer* star Robert August, at one of her favorite Southern California surf spots.

"We never thought of ourselves as pioneers," Poppler says. "I grew up in the Endless Summer era. It was fun, first going up and down the coast and then around the world, surfing and making friends. The environmental activism is all part of it, so that others can enjoy the thrill, adventure and beauty of the ocean."

Debbie Beacham served on the ASP board until 1991. She then moved on to other roles, including a five-year stint in advertising sales with *Surfer* magazine. In 1994, she co-produced with Donna Olson the first all-women surfing 16mm film documentary. It was called *Surfer Girl* and featured Beacham, Frieda Zamba, Jodie Cooper, Pam Burridge and Wendy Botha on a surf trip to Tavarua, Fiji. Against a backdrop of riding perfect reef waves, each woman speaks of her passion for surfing and how each overcame obstacles to pursue her dream. The film won an award at the Chicago International Film Festival in '94 and has been shown since on National Geographic, Discovery International and Outdoor Life Network, among others.

As mother of eight-year-old Alex, and four-year-old Marion, Beacham focuses her energy on her family and on "having fun surfing." She and her husband, Louis, make it a practice to travel with their children. "I want to teach them that the world is bigger than just where we live," she says. Beacham also helps organize the annual Luau and Longboard Invitational each August at Scripps Pier in La Jolla, California, where corporate teams pay to surf with male and female surfing "legends" to benefit the UC-San Diego Cancer Foundation. Each year, the luau raises more than a hundred thousand dollars for cancer research.

Beacham, Poppler and the other women pros of the seventies had vision and tenacity. They laid the groundwork for a stronger, more viable women's pro tour. Veteran surfer and photographer Bernie Baker comments,

"In terms of understanding the ocean, that was the best group of women I've ever seen. You could tell they knew where they were sitting, why they were there and what to do in big water. Everything was focused on Hawaii then, so they had to dive into the winter surf and because of this they shared a special bond. With the women today, Hawaii is just a one-week period in their lives and then they're gone."

Beacham believes the experience, including the struggles, was worth it. "I look at life as though it's made up of chapters. Each one a big part of a great life journey. Surfing taught me many lessons that I'd like to pass along."

Pioneer surfers hold court at San Onofre, 1998: l to r, Joyce Hoffman, Debbie Hull, Linda Davoli, Mary Setterholm, Candi Woodward, Shannon Aikman, Margo Oberg.
Photo: Elizabeth Pepin

The FloJo of Surfing

Frieda Zamba almost gave up surfing at the tender age of nine, when she wiped out and got whacked by a ten-foot board in her home break at Daytona Beach, Florida. She didn't try surfing again for three years. "Then," she says, "I fell in love with it again and got hooked."

Frieda Zamba

She loved it so much that in 1982 at age seventeen she became the youngest woman surfer to win an ASP pro event. An unknown, she burst upon the Mazda Surfsports Pro contest in Solana Beach, California, and blew the competition out of the water. She stunned both the audience and her fellow competitors with her tight, powerful and explosive style, and won effortlessly. She ranks this win as the best moment of her career. "It changed my life," she says, "brought me sponsors and the opportunity of better things to come." Better things such as her first world title, which she won in 1984 at nineteen. In the ten years of her pro career, Zamba won four world titles and countless pro events. Only four other surfers have won four world titles on the ASP circuit, including two women—Wendy Botha and Lisa Andersen, both Zamba's contemporaries.

Zamba had the makings of a champion early on. Her parents encouraged their son and four daughters to participate in sports. A natural athlete, Zamba excelled in basketball and track and field in school. She finally became interested in water sports again when her brother started surfing in 1977. Her earlier wipeout conveniently forgotten, she decided to follow her brother's lead. She learned to surf on borrowed surfboards. The next summer, she mowed lawns to earn enough money to buy her own board for ninety dollars. Her future husband sold it to her.

Flea Shaw was a local pro who owned a surf shop. He also sponsored a surf team, which Zamba joined at age fifteen. She says that her decision to become a pro came about "accidentally" and adds, "I entered a pro/am contest at sixteen, won it, took the money and never looked back." After Zamba won the Mazda Surfsports Pro, Shaw started coaching her seriously. Eventually, he also started courting her. They were married in 1987, the year before she won her fourth world title.

Zamba, her first surfboard and first boyfriend, 1977. Photo: Zamba collection

In the early part of her career, some women pros criticized Zamba for having an unfair advantage with Shaw as her coach. "We were the first to develop the surfer/coach approach to competitive surfing," she says. "The other girls were critical of it because of the advantages that came from it. But it didn't take them long to catch on. Within two years, the top eight girls had coaches or were considering it."

Zamba stayed in shape for surfing by beach running, lap swimming, light-weight training, jumping rope, tennis . . . and surfing. Australian pro Pam Burridge, who finished second to two of Zamba's world titles, called Zamba "the fittest woman on the planet." Burridge recently told *Wahine* magazine, "Frieda was very hard to beat. Not unbeatable, but you were stoked when you managed a win. She was the best athlete. She had a huge impact on the sport and influenced a whole new generation."

World champion Debbie Beacham adds, "Frieda was, and still is, the best woman surfer ever." Current pro Prue Jeffries agrees. "I went on a surf trip with Frieda early in 1999. I think she was thirty-four at the time, and she's better than ever. I told her I was glad she wasn't going to be on tour with us." Jodi Young, surfer, writer and owner of the Ocean Promotion public relations company, calls Zamba the "FloJo of surfing . . . She had an Olympic sprinter's physique [and] a private, on-a-mission kind of presence that elevated her and kept you admiring from a distance." The aloofness that many of Zamba's competitors witnessed was as much a product of intense shyness as of the concentration required to be champion.

Zamba feels she contributed a radical approach to women's surfing. "It wasn't looked at as just a feminine style," she says. "It had some power, aggression and new maneuvers. It was a fresh approach." And it worked in both small and big waves, enabling Zamba to break the stranglehold that longtime champions and big wave experts Margo Oberg and Lynne Boyer had over the tour.

From 1982 through 1984, Zamba considered her fiercest competitor to be Kim Mearig, the tall blonde Californian who took the title in 1983. "Kim was a West Coast girl. The media hype around her was intense and I really shied away from the media then," says Zamba. As she matured, she realized that it was good to have the media on her side. She says, "It opens up a lot of opportunities."

In 1985 and 1986, South African Wendy Botha posed the largest threat. "She had a huge ego," says Zamba, "but her surfing could back it up. My most empowering moment in surfing came when I beat Wendy

Top: Debbie Beacham says, "Frieda Zamba was, and still is, the best woman surfer, ever."
Photo: Jeff Divine

Bottom: Kim Mearig captured the world champion title in 1983, and was one of Zamba's toughest competitors.
Photo: Jim Russi

at Surfer's Paradise in Australia after losing to her repeatedly."

In 1987, Zamba hit a turning point in her career when she went into a slump and lost the world title. She hated being second and vowed not to let it happen again. By then, Burridge was nipping at her heels. "Between 1988 and 1992, Pam could win heats just off of her tactics and experience," says Zamba. "She was a mentally tough competitor."

Zamba regained her title in 1988 and then quit while she was on top. "Once you get to the top, the hardest part is holding on to the title," she says. "I sort of lost the passion. I missed free surfing. I wanted to take some time off." She competed in select events until 1992, winning several major tournaments in the U.S., including the Op (Ocean Pacific) Pro in 1989, 1990 and 1991 and the O'Neill/Pepsi Classic at Santa Cruz in 1990. She retired to the small town of Flagler Beach, Florida, just north of Daytona Beach, because, she says, "I know everybody here, and it's a good place to relax." The town named the Frieda Zamba Aquatic Complex in her honor.

Zamba often surfs Flagler Pier, much to the delight of local surfers and the disapproval of local police, who once arrested her. Flagler Beach law forbids surfing within a few hundred yards of the pier, due to the danger of colliding with pilings. Zamba remembers the day as one of classic surf, with a six-foot swell that produced hollow waves off the pier. "The first wave I got totally barreled and came out," she says. "Then I got arrested, but it was worth it." The host of a local radio talk show mounted a call-in campaign to vote for or against her incarceration. Callers were overwhelmingly in support of Zamba. The charges were eventually dropped.

Unlike famous surf arenas in Australia, California and Hawaii, Florida is not known for near-perfect, dependable waves. Florida surfers commonly vie for small, mushy waves that break near the shore, appropriately called "beach break." Now and then, a hurricane will produce a swell. Or, the weather will converge in exactly the right manner—a low pressure system arrives from the West, the jet stream drops down into the Carolinas, a light westerly wind forms, consistent barometric pressure develops—and create good surf. When

all these factors come together, it's surf nirvana in Florida.

When asked how a place with a reputation for inconsistent surf consistently produces champion surfers, including herself and Lisa Andersen and six-time men's champ Kelly Slater, Zamba replies, "Florida surfers have to adapt to so many conditions that when we do get good surf we surf it for every drop we can. Also, beach break waves break fast for a short distance, requiring you to be very quick and light on your feet. Florida surfers can make a terrible wave look good just because we ride a lot of junk surf and can adapt to conditions more easily than, say, a surfer from Hawaii."

She adds, "We do get some epic days and some insane hurricane swells. It's just all the waiting in between those epic days that's so frustrating. That's the most common surf term heard in Florida—*frustration*."

For someone who could have been a track star and never entered the water, Zamba feels that surfing "opened my eyes to a world I never would have seen otherwise. It has inspired me to work towards my goals and to lead a healthy life." The run-in with the pier police is about as racy as Zamba gets.

Zamba continues her career in surfing as a sales rep for various surf companies. "I appreciate that I can earn a living from surfing, and I cherish the time I spend with my family"—referring to husband Shaw and their "son," a one-hundred-twenty-five-pound Akita named Bear.

Zamba has not lost her passion for the sport and is passing her knowledge on to a new generation. Between April and October each year she works with surf shops, giving clinics up and down the Florida coast. A few years ago, she finally met her surfing inspiration, Larry Bertleman, at a Florida surf trade show and received an autographed photo. "He was such an innovative surfer," says Zamba. "Super radical for his time."

She could be describing herself.

Time out for play. Zamba and her Akita, Bear. Photo: Zamba collection

Photo: Jim Russi

East Coast Wahines Surf On

By Karin Moeller

Long before Floridians Frieda Zamba and Lisa Andersen burst on the surf scene in the eighties and nineties and captured four world titles apiece, Mimi Munro was ripping up the waters of the East Coast, winning regional and state championships wherever she surfed. Munro won the 1965 East Coast Championship at age thirteen in Wrightsville Beach, North Carolina, and followed that up with two more in succeeding years. In 1966, she attended the Makaha International in Hawaii, chaperoned by Joyce Hoffman. Luckily, Hoffman won, so young Munro didn't have to swim home.

"I was so young, I thought of myself like a grain of sand on the beach next to women like Joyce, Joey Hamasaki and Jericho Poppler," says Munro, now a licensed massage therapist and East Coast sales rep for *Wahine* magazine. Unlike Hoffman and her contemporaries, Munro found the notoriety of being a surf star overwhelming. "I was very shy, and I didn't have a good foundation to fall back on at home," she says. "I'd hear kids making derogatory remarks about athletic women surfers. Some of the kids at school were jealous and would threaten me. Some were afraid to approach me because they thought I was stuck up. I wasn't. I was shy. It was a lonely place to be. I realized I had other things in my heart to search out and just stopped showing up at contests."

Munro stopped surfing altogether by fifteen. She married, had two daughters and two sons, divorced and became a single mom. "I don't remember ever missing surfing. I was always near the ocean, which was comforting."

About seven years ago, her seventeen-year-old daughter took up surfing. After being awakened at night by dreams about surfing, Munro followed her daughter into the water. Munro says she surfs better now, at age forty-eight, than she did as a kid. "I appreciate it more, now that I'm more comfortable with myself."

Even so, Munro says it took forever to introduce herself to her neighbors, Andersen and Zamba. Munro and Andersen both live in Ormond Beach; Zamba is about fifteen minutes north in Flagler Beach. "Lisa and I just wave at each other," says Munro. "She's about as shy as I am."

East Coast champion Mimi Munro, mid-1960s. Photo: LeRoy Grannis

Three years ago, Munro began teaching at Surf Camp through the local lifeguard association. Zamba often attends as guest instructor. "When I started surfing, Frieda was maybe two years old," says Munro. "Now she's coaching another up-and-coming Florida surfer, Falina Spires."

As East Coast sales rep for *Wahine*, Munro attends many contests along the Eastern seaboard, including the East Coast Wahine Championships in Wrightsville Beach, North Carolina, an all-girl contest that debuted in 1997. The event, originally organized by Tammy Kennedy, is now coordinated by her friend Anne Beasley, whom she met surfing in the Eastern Surfing Association (ESA). "It was a real grassroots event. It started with seventy-six girls, mostly locals," says Beasley. "People came in from the ESA and volunteered to help run the contest. In 1998, the number grew to one hundred fifteen and, by 1999, the tally reached one hundred seventy-six."

The two-day contest, held in August, attracts wahines of all ages from across the Eastern seaboard. Participants enjoy prizes and a grand banquet with live music, a fashion show and slide show. "We've never been blessed with good surf, but we're East Coasters so we know that it's all a gamble," says Beasley. "And we've got little girls, just seven years old, who are so inspired. I can guarantee you that there's more girls surfing Wrightsville Beach than anywhere—just because of the contest."

The event's web site, www.eastcoastwahines.com, posts past contest results and photos and provides directions, hotel information, entry forms and even a chat room. "The chat room is great for networking women up and down the coast who have a common interest in surfing and the water lifestyle. The whole idea is to build a community so these women won't feel alone."

In addition to coordinating the contest, Beasley is an ambassador for Water Girl apparel company, a guest instructor at Surf Diva in La Jolla and a freelance writer who pens articles for *Surfer, Surfing Girl, Surfing* and *Eastern Surf Magazine.*

"When the contest happens and it's Friday night and all those girls pull into town and there are seventy-five girls surfing at the pier and all the guys are, like, 'What is going on?' it's like a party in the water," says Beasley.

Competitors at the East Coast Wahine Championships, 1999. Photo: Courtesy Anne Beasley

"And it's not so much about the competition. It's really about a weekend of women coming together, surfing together, sharing waves, sharing laughs and sharing friendships. Everyone goes home with a big smile on her face."

Munro adds: "I love it. I meet little girls to women my age and older. We surf together and talk. I let them know that I'm no different than they are, just because I was a champion. Some girls are still coming to terms with their athleticism and femininity. I want them to understand that it's more accepted now for a woman to be an athlete."

Thanks to Munro, Beasley and their fellow East Coast surfers, the women's surf beat goes on.

The East Coast Wahine Championships
inspires a new generation of wahines.
Photo: Courtesy Anne Beasley

Photo: Jim Russi

Growing Up on Tour

The first professional female surfer in Australia won an amateur competition at age twelve. Quiet but driven, Pam Burridge of Sydney turned pro in 1982 at age sixteen, determined to be the best surfer in the world. Highly talented and adored by the Australian press, Burridge seemed poised to achieve her dream. But it was not to be: A maelstrom of self-doubt, rebellion and identity crises engulfed her and nearly dashed her hopes.

Burridge discovered surfing at age ten. She talked her parents into buying her a five-foot-eight single-fin board. A "goofy-footer" (riding with her right foot forward), she took to the sport with a passion. For the first few years, the tall, skinny blonde in a wetsuit wasn't even recognized as a girl by other surfers. When she was twelve, her mother took her to the Manly Pacific Boardrider's Contest at North Steyne Beach, where Burridge entered the only women's heat. Her goal was to not come in last. In Marion Stell's 1992 biography, Burridge recalls: "I had no idea what you had to do to win a surf contest, so I just paddled out with the others and caught every wave I could." She won.

Pam Burridge

Burridge joined as many amateur contests as possible, often surfing against the boys. By 1979, when she was fourteen, she was attracting both media coverage and sponsors. In the 1980 season alone she won six amateur titles. That year, she and two other Australian women surfers, Sharon Holland and Pru Howarth, were invited to compete in the Offshore Women's Masters and the Op Women's World Cup in Hawaii. There, Burridge was awestruck, watching all the famous-name surfers prepare—including world champions Margo Oberg and Lynne Boyer. Burridge surfed well, came in fifth and achieved a professional ranking of eleventh in the world.

The Australian media predicted that Burridge would be the Margo Oberg of the 1980s. At such a young age, it was easy for Burridge to fall into the trap of believing her own publicity. Whenever she failed to score high in a contest, her already low self-esteem would be intensified by the feeling that she was failing to live up to the expectations of the press. At the time, no Australian woman had become world champion, and the media was clamoring for an Aussie to break the American women's stranglehold.

Because Burridge's sense of self-worth was tied to whether or not she won contests, she found herself on a continual emotional roller coaster. She altered her appearance. At one point, she cut off her long blonde hair, dyed it pink and tangerine and kept it cropped short. "I wanted to be a punk or a rebel, but at the same time I was trying to sell my image, so it was 'What am I doing here?' I was looking the part of someone who didn't want to

play the game." The California surf girl look was coming on strong, Burridge adds. "They all had long blonde hair and classic figures and tans and wore swim suits. The surfie girl tag labeled me a bit more than I would have liked."

She looked for escape in drugs and alcohol, easy to find in both her surfing and music circles (her recording, "Summertime All Round the World," became a hit single in 1984). Burridge states, "At first, it was a fun thing. You'd go to the pub with your friends and have a few drinks. Somewhere it shifted and turned into a thing that didn't make me happy. It fueled my doubt and self-loathing, and it fueled my view of the world as mean and bleak."

She drifted in and out of alcohol and drug recovery programs, while at the same time exhibiting an awesome surfing style against the best women of the era. In 1982, she came within two contest wins of capturing the world title, the year that Californian Debbie Beacham was crowned world champ at age twenty-nine. Burridge says that she's glad she didn't win the world title at such a young age: "I wasn't mature enough to cope with the winning."

Until 1983, Burridge was an upstart competing mostly against older women, including Oberg, Boyer, Poppler, Sunn and Beacham: the first generation of professional women surfers. In a 1983 *Los Angeles Times* article, Poppler said of Burridge: "Pam is one of the most dynamic individuals of the new guard in surfing. Her style is aggressive. Her technique is crisp and dramatic with staccato-like movements. She incorporates the new wave of surfing technique."

A new wave of pros broke into the circuit in 1983, including Floridian Frieda Zamba and Californian Kim Mearig. Both became Burridge's fiercest rivals. Burridge called the next few years "the Kim and Frieda Show." She added, "I had to turn around and surf against seventeen-year-olds like me, and they were really good, and they were touring the world, so the scene changed a lot." Mearig won the title in 1983, followed by Zamba, who captured an unprecedented four world titles between 1984 and 1988. During this time, Burridge managed to finish second four times, and only once slipped below third.

In 1984, Jodie Cooper from Western Australia made her pro debut and quickly proved herself a gutsy surfer. Another newcomer, South African Wendy Botha (who would eventually adopt Australian citizenship in order to bypass anti-apartheid contest restrictions), also posed a threat. By the end of the year, Aussies Toni

Burridge's crisp and dramatic movements introduced
"a new wave of surfing technique."
Photo: Jim Russi

Sawyer and Jenny Gill had also turned pro. In 1987, another Aussie rookie, Pauline Menczer, entered the tour and knocked out Burridge in the very first round of a title-cinching contest at Manly Beach. After that, the Australian press turned up the pressure for an Aussie girl to win the title. Burridge, at nineteen, was no longer the ingénue. In the media's eye, she was a mature surfer who should be winning.

The irony was that she *was* winning. Burridge upset her competitors in contest after contest, but she always came up shy of enough points to cinch the number one spot.

During the 1987 season, Burridge was more occupied with becoming "clean and sober" and getting her life together than with winning the world title. That year, in Hawaii, she became run-down and sick. She was befriended by another pro woman surfer, who had recovered from alcohol and drug problems several years earlier. According to Burridge, "It helped to listen to someone who was just like me, with the same sort of past, telling me what happened to her and how she felt and how she got well. From then on, I was free to recover. It was definitely the turning point in my life. I started to go to meetings and be part of a recovery program, as opposed to a sitting-on-the-fence program."

That year, Burridge also fell to seventh in the top sixteen pro rankings. Ironically, the slip enabled her to break free of the pressure to be number one. The next season, back and in top form, she began her climb up the

Photo: Jim Russi

ranks. The competition was incredibly fierce: there were old rivals Zamba, Mearig, Cooper and Botha; Menczer, now with one pro season under her belt; and added threats from hot Californians Jorja and Jolene Smith, and newcomer Lisa Andersen from Florida. Veterans Oberg and Boyer could be counted upon to make the Hawaiian leg of the tour particularly difficult. The final ratings for '88 gave Zamba the world title, Burridge second place, Botha third, Cooper fourth and Menczer fifth. The Aussie newspapers proclaimed, "Burridge Is Bridesmaid Once Again." But Burridge was happy, having risen from seventh to second in one year.

In 1989, Burridge focused on fitness training and relaxation techniques. She also developed a relationship with veteran surfer and shaper Mark Rabbidge. Rabbidge began shaping boards for Burridge's height, weight and surfing style. They shared a love of surfing and eventually of each other.

Burridge retained second place in 1989, while Botha took the world title. At that point, Rabbidge sat her down and asked her point-blank to decide if she really wanted to win the world title in 1990. He felt that she had come to a crossroads where she needed to decide to go for it or "forget it and go soul surfing." Burridge said, "I want to go for it."

For the 1990 season, Rabbidge took over the business side of Burridge's career, leaving her free to surf. Her plan was to give no media interviews before major contests, easing the pressure. The competitive field was

strong: Botha, Menczer, Cooper, Mearig, Aussie rookies Michele Donoghoe and Neridah Falconer, and Americans Alicia Schwarzstein and Lisa Andersen. The press was already calling Andersen "the best woman surfer in the world," but she had yet to win a professional contest. Burridge considered Andersen one of her biggest threats: "She was looking like she was going to hit top form and spoil all my plans." Zamba, who was by then semiretired, entered only one event and then returned to Florida.

By the end of the season, the title had come down to one contest: the Underwets Women's Pro at Hawaii's Sunset Beach. Burridge had won the contest the year before, which gave her an edge, but the pressure was on as never before. Things started happening in Burridge's favor. First, Andersen failed to advance to the semifinals. Then, her closest rival in ranking, Botha, was knocked out in a semifinal heat. Burridge suddenly realized that she had a shot at the title.

The final heat pitted Burridge against her friends and fellow Aussies Menczer, Cooper and Sawyer—none of whom gave her an inch of advantage. Burridge had to depend on technique and experience. With fifteen seconds to go, she caught the winning wave. At age twenty-five, after a decade of wrestling with her competitiveness and self-doubt, the World Champion title came as an especially sweet reward.

Burridge with her OP Pro trophy, 1984. Photo: Debbie Beacham collection

Burridge continued to compete through 1993 with a new attitude: "My life is no longer validated by the results of a surfing competition. I made a decision to love myself regardless and to try to care for myself as a higher power would like me to. I'm not going to punish myself for not winning, because there's not much difference between winning and losing as far as performance goes."

She and Rabbidge married in 1993. Burridge competed in Australian tournaments through 1996 and then reentered the world tour in 1997. "It was the first time I had traveled and competed against girls who were nearly half my age," she says. "I forgot that I had been fifteen on tour." After having a baby in 1999, she decided not to travel and allowed her seeding in the pro rankings to expire. "I felt a twinge of sadness," she admits, "but also of relief."

Burridge believes that she has contributed to women gaining acceptance in surfing, not only in Australia but also worldwide. "I'd like to think that because my career lasted a long time, other women surfers will be encouraged and also have long careers. I'd like to think I've opened the door for a more inclusive approach to the sport."

Burridge "still gets a bit fired up in the surf" and plans to be a lifelong surfer. "I can't imagine not being out there. I still surf every chance I get, especially after having the baby. We live in a coastal country town, so Isobel will be at the beach and she will surf, if she wants to."

But, no pressure.

Fellow Aussie Jodie Cooper was an
awesome rival. Photo: Jim Russi

The Legacy of Isobel Letham

In 1915, Australia invited Olympic swimming champion Duke Kahanamoku to the land "down under" to put on speed-swimming exhibitions. It just so happened that the famous Hawaiian, like many of his fellow beach boys in Waikiki, was also an expert surfer.

On Saturday, a crowd formed on the beach at Manly to watch the legendary waterman. In the crowd was Isobel Letham, a fifteen-year-old rough water swimmer from Freshwater. Inspired by the feats of Australian Olympians Fanny Durack and Mina Wylie, Letham was described by the local press as "an Australian girl swimmer who only comes out of the surf to eat and sleep."

Letham had a reason for being there other than her interest in swimming. Duke Kahanamoku had not brought his own surfboard to Australia, so he had asked Isobel's father, a local builder, to help him make one from a plank of sugar pine. The board weighed over seventy-five pounds. Letham described it as "about as big as the bottom of a boat."

Duke paddled out from the beach, farther than swimmers normally ventured. He caught wave after wave and thrilled the crowd—standing, kneeling, doing headstands on his board, somersaulting at the end of a ride. In Duke's own words, he "soared and glided, drifted and sideslipped, with that blend of flying and sailing which only experienced surfers can know and fully appreciate. The Aussies became instant converts."

Duke wanted a young woman to paddle out with him and Letham, standing front and center in the crowd, was chosen. "When we caught a wave, I was terrified," she later recalled. "It was like going over a cliff." Terrified, yes—but hooked. That summer she became the proud owner of another surfboard made by her father. Isobel had a second reason not to come out of the surf.

Throughout the early twentieth century, Australian women (and men) followed Letham's lead and taught themselves to surf. In travel brochures for Australia, surfing was an advertised leisure activity. By the early sixties, surfing was appealing to women in Hawaii, California, Florida and Australia. When the first world amateur surfing championship was held at Manly Beach in 1964, Australian Phyllis O'Donnell won the title.

In 1978, several women surfers unhappy with the treatment that women's surfing was receiving from male officials formed their own group, the Australian Women's Surfriders Association (AWSA). Isobel Letham, still actively promoting the sport at age seventy-eight, was selected as AWSA's patron. At a surfing event, Letham was introduced to a shy twelve-year-old being heralded by the press as the best among the rising stars in women's surfing: Pam Burridge. Burridge was impressed by Letham's "devil may care attitude. She was like a teenager in an elderly lady."

Letham lived to see Burridge win the world title. In 1999, Burridge named her first daughter after the woman who had pioneered surfing in Australia.

Fourteen-year-old Burridge with Isobel Letham, Australia's
first surfer, 1980. Photo: Pam Burridge collection

"I try to open my eyes and see what's going on around me."
Photo: Tom Servais

If it weren't for her toughness and reality-based approach to life, Lisa Andersen's story would read almost like a fairy tale.

Lisa Andersen

Andersen grew up a troubled and rebellious child, caught in the turmoil of her parents' disintegrating marriage. She sought escape in surfing and, as her mother recalls, "gave me more trouble than any of her three brothers." Her parents disapproved of the sport and tried to dissuade her. Her father even went so far as to break one of her surfboards. "Mom and Dad thought surfing was bums at the beach smoking marijuana," says Andersen. "Surfing was not something that a young lady should be doing." But surfing was all that Andersen wanted to do.

Naturally athletic, at age ten she was the only girl on the Little League team in Fork Union, Virginia. In 1982, after the family moved to Daytona Beach, Florida, thirteen-year-old Andersen switched her attention to the beach. "I went to a junior high school where the whole fashion thing was Sundek baggies and Op walk shorts. I wanted to be in fashion with everybody else," she says. "Then I realized there were people out in the water surfing. So I borrowed a board and taught myself to surf. I used to stand up with both feet side by side, knees knocked. I learned the hard way." She also earned the nickname Trouble for harassing the guys in the water with her aggressive style.

She joined her high school surfing team—the only girl—and started skipping school to ride the waves and to avoid going home to her parents' fighting. This did not go over well with her parents, who considered having Andersen placed under house arrest for truancy. Before that could happen, Andersen bolted. She didn't simply hide out at a girlfriend's house, waiting for the storm to blow over. Andersen used money from summertime odd jobs and bought a one-way plane ticket to Los Angeles. She left her mother a note: "I'm leaving to become the world champion of women's surfing."

Andersen recalls that she wasn't certain there was such a title. "I had to say something that would make an impact," she says. "I wanted my mother to know that I was serious."

Only sixteen, Andersen drifted to Huntington Beach, known to surf fanatics as Surf City, USA. Its pier hosts the prestigious U.S. Surfing Championships contest

Lisa and daughter Erica with an eye to the future. Photo: Jim Russi

each summer. The streets are lined with surf shops, surfing history—and surf bums. By 1985, when Andersen arrived, the town's seedy sixties' drug culture patina was not quite as visible, but a young girl still could get into trouble.

Andersen didn't. The surfing community became the nurturing, protective "family" that she sought. "It's all I ever saw myself doing and someone in a higher place knew that and took care of me," she states. "I know anything could have happened to me. I was only sixteen, but I met the right people. They took care of me and guided me through different levels."

This is not to say that she didn't go through some hard times. As she says, "Every young girl does. Falls in love, meets people and gets hurt, confidence gets shattered." Andersen waited tables, worked at a surf shop and surfed. In between places to live, she slept on the beach under the pier.

One famous story involves Ian Cairns, a former pro surfer and founder of the ASP pro circuit. In 1986, just before the start of a National Scholastic Surfing Association (NSSA) contest, he found Andersen asleep under a table. When she awoke, she asked to compete. Cairns, perhaps recognizing a familiar, intense hunger in young Andersen's eyes, fudged the rules a bit (she was not attending school at the time) and let her in. She won.

Fairy tale beauty awakens and her dream comes true?

Not exactly. Andersen did go on to sweep the amateur circuit, bringing home thirty-five trophies in an eight-month stretch. She turned pro at age seventeen and joined the world tour. The media started watching, and the pressure began. "When I turned pro, suddenly it was really hard for me to see myself winning," she says. "I struggled for a long time. I couldn't get through heats. I would get out of trial heats, but I had trouble in the one-on-one heats. I had all these Little League dads around me, one telling me to do one thing, the other telling me something else. The direction wasn't coming from inside me."

It all clicked into place seven years later, Andersen says, after she gave birth to her daughter, Erica. In 1992, Andersen had just been picked up by her current sponsor, Quiksilver/Roxy, and was surfing at Jeffrey's Bay in South Africa. Knowing she had a flight to catch, she hopped one last wave, and, harking back to her days as Trouble, cut off Renato Hickel, the head ASP judge who was also out enjoying some free surfing. She gave him a friendly wave, finished her ride and then ran off to the airport.

Watch out photographers, here
comes Trouble. Photo: Jim Russi

Hickel, a tall, handsome Brazilian, soon caught up with Andersen during a contest at Reunion Island. She ended up dancing with him at a post-surf party. Their slightly controversial romance—Hickel had to give up judging women's heats—produced Erica.

Andersen married Hickel early in 1993, but after Erica was born in August she began to lose interest in the marriage. They separated in 1996. Hickel is still an ASP official and often sees his daughter and Andersen on the tour. They are friendly. "I just had to move on," says Andersen. She is, ultimately, a loner. "I work better alone. I can't have a husband, boyfriend or anyone telling me what to do."

She competed while pregnant with Erica. "I had just signed with Quiksilver. I had convinced them to believe in me, and then I got pregnant. They were like, 'Great, now what?' So I ended up competing that year and missing only one event, during my last term of pregnancy. I finished seventh overall."

With Erica to care for, surfing became a serious career, says Andersen. "I didn't have time to be just a nomad on the tour. I had a family. Erica kept me focused on what I had to do. She distracted me from the partying, talking to people and not visualizing or focusing on the surf.

Photo: Jim Russi

"I started to see myself on the podium. Then I had this enormous amount of strength that came after giving birth to Erica. I've talked to other women athletes who've had children, and many have told me that they had their best efforts after childbirth. Childbirth is not fun, but it's the most womanly thing you can ever experience and then, afterwards, you're invincible."

This seemed true as Andersen began mowing down the competition. Between 1994 and 1997, she won four successive world titles. Her fame catapulted her beyond the contest scene and surfing press to the general

public, who seemed captivated by the juxtaposition of her natural beauty and fierce competitive style. Then, midway through the 1998 season, a herniated disc shattered the fairy tale.

She had begun having back troubles in the eighties. "I think I was born with back problems, but they didn't start to show up until I was nineteen or twenty," she says. "After I had Erica, there was so much going on: Having her with me on tour, the pressure of competition, of wanting to do well for my sponsors. When I won the title in 1994, the pressure was instantly lifted. I had been pursuing the title for eight years and the pain went away. It was a spiritual moment."

Near the end of the next season, Andersen was far ahead in points when "something snapped" in her back. "I was doing an MTV sports program in Brazil, and I just kept going," she says. "I didn't want to disappoint them." She ended up being carried out of the event on a stretcher. Luckily, her lead was so great that she only had to advance out of the quarter-final heat in the final event of the season to retain her title. She accomplished this feat in great pain.

By the beginning of the following season, the pain had disappeared again. She managed the injury well enough to hold on to the world title through 1997. Then she was knocked out of the tour with the herniated disc and severe sciatica. She took off the rest of 1998 and all of 1999 to recuperate and focus on 2000 as a comeback year.

"I've thought a lot about whether or not I want to go backwards and start all over again," she says. "I had to leave with an injury. That's not the way I want to end my career. I figure 2000 is my chance to end it with winning or not winning, but competing a full year without injury."

Andersen draws upon an inner strength that also acts as a protective shell. She has been called "shy," but after fifteen years of being in the public eye, and for the last six years being the object of more superlatives than any other female surfer (and many male surfers) in history, it's easy to understand her reticence. She has been hounded by autograph seekers and even stalked by a French radio journalist. She is named "favorite surfer" year

Andersen's style is aggressive, fast, strong, fluid
and influential. Photo: Jim Russi

SURFER

Photo Annual

Lisa Andersen surfs
better than you.

Display Until December 18, 1995

02 >

0 74470 01528 4

U.S. $3.99 CANADA $4.50
FEBRUARY '96 VOL. 37 NO. 2

after year in polls of aspiring girl surfers. There have been other famous women surfers, but none has attained the celebrity of Lisa Andersen.

In 1995, *Surfer* featured Andersen on its cover with the line, "Lisa Andersen surfs better than you." Afterwards, Bob Hurley, then head of the surf apparel company Billabong made a T-shirt that read, "I surf like Lisa."

"There's no way I can look at it in a bad way. My heroes were all guys," she says. "To me, it means I was doing something here." Her surfing heroes were Tom Curren, Barton Lynch, Mark Richards, Shaun Tomson and Mark Occhilupo. "These were the guys I read about and watched. I remember looking through the fence at the Op Pro and being dumbfounded." When she first saw Pam Burridge and Kim Mearig surfing at Huntington Beach, she was intimidated. "I'd just go out and get in their way." Later, she admired the style of fellow-Floridian Zamba, although she commented that she least liked to surf against Zamba because "she is the ultimate competitor."

Andersen's surfing is aggressive, fast, strong, fluid—and influential. She and her peers know that she has raised the performance bar in women's surfing. Rochelle Ballard comments, "When you surf with Lisa, you find yourself smoothing out your own surfing. Her technique is so refined that it rubs off on everybody around her."

The famous *Surfer* cover.
Photo: Tom Dugan, courtesy *Surfer*

Andersen is especially interested in influencing the younger set. "I knew from the beginning that I wasn't going to settle for the label of 'Yeah, she's pretty good for a girl.' It's good to see a lot of the younger girls following in the same path. When I see my picture on their wall and when they come up to me for an autograph, I know I'm having a positive effect. That's satisfying. I go to Roxy amateur contests and see hundreds of little girls ripping on all different kinds of boards. All of them are just so stoked to be a part of the beach lifestyle."

Andersen and her mother reconciled several years ago. Andersen recently bought a home in Florida and invited her mother to move in. The stability has been good for daughter, mother and grandmother. "Erica has her own room, her own bed, she's in school and learning how to read," says Andersen.

But here's the blight on a perfect happy ending: "I need to spend more time with Erica, but suddenly I'm going away on tour again. My mother used to take care of Erica, but now my mother's become deaf, so I can't communicate with her while I'm away. I worry about that."

Only at times. Andersen has a handle on fear, gained from years of surfing. "Fear turns into adrenaline and energy, if you let it," she says. "I have different ways of dealing with fear." She seems to drift away as she speaks: "When there's a big wave coming and I'm caught inside, I just let my board go. It's still attached to me by the leg rope, but I go down as far as I can and then roll around on my back and look up with my eyes open. It's actually beautiful, you see everything floating over you. The wave pulls you into the turbulence of the whitewash, but, at the same time, you relax, and then you see when it's okay to surface."

She sits up, blinking. "I try to do stuff like that, open my eyes and see what's going on around me."

Barrel Ballard

In 1987, Kauai's local paper published a story about a sixteen-year-old surfer, Rochelle Ballard. She was asked to name her goals in life. "I said, 'To become world champion and to help change the face of women's surfing,'" Ballard recounts. "My grandmother framed the article and still has it on her wall. Seeing it now, I think that's cool. When you're young, you want to do everything. To be able to stick with something gives you a life purpose."

Ballard grew up on Kauai surfing, biking and skateboarding with the guys. She began competing in amateur contests at age fourteen while working in her parents' restaurant. "I'd just barely make it to work on time, my hair still wet," she says. "I'd be so stoked from surfing. I never had that 'Yuck, back at work' attitude."

Ballard pulls into a big one, her specialty. Photo: Jim Russi

A nine-year veteran of the pro circuit, Ballard has yet to capture the crown, but she has no regrets. "I love surfing, period," she says. "My sponsors are really supportive of me. They let me be who I am and don't put any pressure on me for my contest results. It's all about my surfing and the exposure I get."

She gets plenty. Her five-foot-one frame is petite but muscular. Her demeanor is gutsy. She is the acknowledged queen of barrel-riding. The ultimate feat in surfing, barrel-riding requires a wave with a lip that curls over and forms a tube—or barrel—big enough for the surfer to get inside so that she can ride the face of the wave while the lip peels off overhead. "You're in the barrel and there's this quiet rumble, there's so much energy in that rumble, the sound of the ocean's power," says Ballard. "To be inside that sound is to be inside the energy source of the wave."

Her other forte is championing women's surfing. For four years, she served on the ASP board, helping to direct, and redirect, the future of women's professional surfing. "Women's surfing has gone through its growing pains," she states. "The future is exciting. The circuit is going to have a new face, with separate events for women. I've worked hard for it, and I've done it for the young girls coming up, not for myself."

At the end of the 1999 season, Ballard resigned her board position to give herself more time to surf and to start a family with her husband, surf cinematographer Bill

Ballard. "I'll probably be on the tour for one more year. It's been a great life," she says at the ripe old age of twenty-nine. "I'm ready for the next phase."

Ballard has helped change the face of women's surfing.
Photo: Jim Russi

113

Billabong Team Rider Layne Beachley on a
30-foot tow-in wave, 1998. Photo: Art Brewer

The Aussie Invasion

Ever since Isobel Letham first propelled surfing to popularity in 1915 and Phyllis O'Donnell captured the first world amateur championship in 1964, Australian women have been formidable competitors.

After the pro tour was initiated in 1976, four Aussie women captured world titles—Wendy Botha, Pam Burridge, Pauline Menczer and Layne Beachley. Botha won the title in 1987, lost it to Frieda Zamba in 1988, regained it in 1989, lost it to Burridge in 1990, regained it in 1991 and held onto it in 1992. In 1993, Menczer took the title. Then Lisa Andersen vaulted to the top and stayed there until June 1998, when her back injury forced her to exit the tour. That year, Beachley moved into first place. In 1999, she repeated her title win.

Layne Beachley

Beachley had been in danger of taking on the media's nickname of "bridesmaid" from Pam Burridge. In 1994, when Andersen began her run, Beachley had finished fourth in overall rankings, then moved to second in 1995, third in 1996 and second again in 1997. "The reason I finally won the world title," she says, "is because I stopped focusing on surfing big waves. My fear was small surf. I had to change my strategy and learn how to surf small waves."

Beachley's style revolves around power. "I get more of an adrenaline rush out of surfing big waves than just surfing in general," she says. "When there's power behind me, I don't have to put so much power into the wave; it's already under my feet. I can just generate my technique without having to concentrate on placing myself in a position on a wave where I can get the most power out of a turn."

and the Girls from Down Under

Beachley grew up in Manly Beach. Her mother died in 1978 when she was six. She started surfing at age three with her dad and brother, but didn't see the sport as a profession until her teens. "I was always a tomboy, played all sorts of sports—cricket, soccer, basketball, softball. I used to hang out with thirteen guys." A skinny grommet (the nickname given to young surfers), Beachley nevertheless earned the reputation of being scrappy and cocky. "The surfers were very territorial," she says. "If we went up to North Steyne Beach, we'd get kicked back

1999 World Champion Beachley.
Photo: Andrea Gabbard

to New Steyne. They'd say, 'You're a girl, what are you doing up here?'"

Beachley was literally, and regularly, thrown off the beach. "They'd pick me up by my wrists and ankles and heave me over the beach wall. I'd get right up, run back over the wall and give as good as I got—and get thrown over again. This would sometimes happen two or three times a day. I think that had a lot to do with who I am now."

Who she is now is Queen of the Hill, and a target. "It's a lot of work being world champion," she says. "It's so much easier being number two. No one comes up to you and says, 'You suck, you don't deserve to be world champion.' Or, 'You shouldn't have won today, you weren't on.' When you're number two, everyone gives you encouragement. They say, 'You can do it, you're the greatest, you deserve to be there.' I've learned not to take these things personally. I remember when I was number two, wanting to take Lisa out. That's what makes a true champion, being able to stay there, handle the criticism, the ridicule and the attention."

These days, in addition to pursuing another world title, Beachley is expanding her parameters through tow-in surfing. Her coach and mentor—and boyfriend—is none other than big-wave legend (and tow-in expert) Ken Bradshaw. They motor out on a jet ski a half mile or more offshore, to where huge waves form in deep water

and break over the outer reefs. There, Layne grabs a rope attached to the jet ski and Ken tows her into the face of a heaving monster. Once she lets go of the rope, she's on the wave, and on her own. As of December 1998, the largest wave she has surfed is a thirty-footer at a place called Backyards.

Beachley is also one of five pro women who have formed a business committee within the ASP to promote women's surfing. "Rochelle Ballard, Megan Abubo, Kate Skarratt, Prue Jeffries and I are concentrating on ways to market and grow our sport," Beachley says. "We feel that the women's circuit is a desirable, marketable commodity."

Skarratt and Jeffries are also Aussies. In fact, of the top

Top: Kate Skarrat.
Photo: Jim Russi

Bottom: Melanie Redman.
Photo: Jim Russi

fourteen women on the ASP 2000 roster, nine hail from Australia. 1999 marked Skarratt's first year on the WCT and Jeffries' sixth. "I'd like to see the sport grow, both as a pro sport and also as a healthy pastime for young women," says Jeffries, a tall, poised, twenty-eight-year-old who joined the tour at age seventeen. "Surfing is such a free sport, it's really as much an art form as a sport. Surfers think about it day in and day out. It's our passion. There are so many constraints in a contest; it limits people's expression on a wave and makes it hard for some surfers to show their true talents. I'd like to be part of the organization that elevates the whole profile, extends performance levels and encourages more girls to get in the water."

Skarratt took over Rochelle Ballard's position on the ASP board in 2000. Unlike many pros, Skarratt finished college first and then entered the tour. She learned to surf while attending university in Woolongong. "I had a real passion for it right away and surfed as often as I could," she says. Her peers also inspire her. "Each of the girls on tour has something I look up to."

Skarratt's goal is "to be the best I can be and to fully express myself in surfing." She adds: "There's something inside me telling me that by traveling around and letting my surfing speak for itself, there's some way that I can help people. In the meantime, I want to help more young women get involved in the sport, through

Prue Jeffries. Photo: Jim Russi

camps, amateur programs and a structure that will make it easier for women to get started."

Other strong Aussie contenders are Serena Brooke, Trudy Todd and Neridah Falconer. Twenty-four-year-old Brooke grew up in Queensland, Australia and advanced from ninth in 1997 to second both in 1998 and 1999, taking over Beachley's "bridesmaid" position. Brooke started surfing at age fourteen and turned pro in 1995. "You grow up quickly on tour," she says. "You're gone for weeks, sometimes months at a time. You slowly wean yourself of having to go home, and you just go with the flow. When I do go home, I drive my car and see as many friends as possible. I bought a house last year so that I'd have some sort of normal life after the tour."

Brooke's surfing mentor was Botha. "I looked up to Lisa, Pam and Pauline, but I went to a surf school where Wendy Botha was teaching and she really inspired me." Brooke's slender physique and cherubic face do not reflect her toughness in the water. Considered a "power surfer," she is aggressive and tenacious—and bal-

anced. "I get energy from the ocean," she says. "Contest surfing can make you feel on top of the world or totally bummed out. I try not to dwell on losing a heat, or a world title. I just try harder the next time."

Trudy Todd, also from Queensland, is a five-foot-two blonde surfing bombshell. Explosive in big waves, Todd also charges the small stuff. She won the 1999 Triple Crown in Hawaii, where the final event was staged in six-to-ten-foot Sunset Beach surf. Todd, twenty-six, has been competing on tour for seven years and says she is just beginning to get into the groove. "There are so many variables to deal with," she says. "The flights, jet lag, different waves, judges, the organization,

Top: Four-time World Champion, Wendy Botha. Photo: Jeff Divine

Bottom: Trudy Todd. Photo: Jim Russi

sponsors, managers. Nowadays, you won't see anyone win a world title under the age of twenty-five. It takes that long to put it all together."

Neridah Falconer is a lithe, athletic thirty-year-old with sun-streaked brown hair. She's a ten-year veteran of the tour and consistently places high in the rankings. "I was fifteen when I started surfing. Where I came from in New South Wales, there were no other girl surfers. I knew who Pam Burridge was. I watched pro events. But I didn't model myself after anyone. I developed my own image."

The women would like to see sponsors acknowledge their individuality. Neridah explains: "With the men, the sponsors play off their images, whether they're rebels or whatever. I'd like to see them do that with the women. Individuality is so important. We're all so different."

Todd adds: "The sponsorship support from the industry has gotten stronger, but there are still some women near the top of the ladder without any support. Take Melanie Redman, in third place in 1999 and no sponsors. Lynette MacKenzie is one of the best surfers on tour, but no sponsorship to speak of. The industry has to get away from the image of a blonde, fourteen-year-old girl running down the beach. There are so many different personalities in the sport, why not celebrate the diversity?"

Serena Drooko. Photo: Jim Russi

Pauline Menczer Holds a Steady Course

After thirteen years on the pro tour without sponsorship, one wonders what keeps twenty-nine-year-old Pauline Menczer going.

She explains that it's her great love for the sport. "Three years ago, I wanted to quit. Now, seeing things change for the women's tour has made me want to stay for many more years. The sport is in the process of a positive blooming."

Menczer believes that she hasn't found a sponsor all these years because she doesn't fit the marketing image of the blue-eyed blonde or the stereotypical Hawaiian. Menczer is short, compact, brunette and freckled. "I am who I am," she says, "and if you don't want to take me as I am, then that's too bad—I miss out."

She hasn't missed out on winning, though. Menczer has captured twenty career victories in addition to the 1993 World Championship. She has earned enough prize money to pay her expenses on tour. A couple years ago, she put a down payment on a small house in Australia, which enabled her to stop living out of her van.

Menczer began surfing at age thirteen on a hand-me-down board from her brother. She had few role models to emulate. "When I first started, it was very rare to see an article about a woman surfer," she says. "I remember seeing an article about Jodie Cooper and Pam Burridge. Those two were the only women surfers I knew existed. It's nice now that people are beginning to know more of the girls on tour."

Menczer agrees that exposure for women's surfing has been increasing. She feels that Lisa Andersen's fame has helped boost media coverage and sponsorship opportunities for women on tour. "Lisa's a fantastic surfer, she's got great ability: four times world champion, I mean what more can you say? Every woman surfer needs that sort of backing."

Aussie surfers, male and female, receive less financial support than their American counterparts. "Americans have better support because it's a bigger country," says Menczer. "Any American girl surfer on tour is pretty much set for sponsorship. Most of the Australian girls are still struggling. Only a few have broken through into the American market. The support coming out of Australia is really pretty pathetic, even though we currently dominate the sport."

All this is not sour grapes. Menczer is just unabashedly honest. She is quite well liked on the tour and is known for her go-for-it surfing in all wave conditions. People admire her for having endured a debilitating rheumatoid arthritis since her teens.

To stay in shape and to keep her joints flexible, she says, "I just surf as much as I can. I've spent my whole life dealing with arthritis, so I've never really had a strict schedule of doing certain training. It depends on how I feel. I've always felt that swimming helps a lot, and it doesn't hurt. So sometimes I do that. When I'm really into

training, I'm surfing a lot and feel like I don't have to do much more than that. When I'm home, I do a lot of gardening. I live on a steep hill. Pushing a wheelbarrow up the hill is a good workout."

Menczer is satisfied with her lifestyle and feels fortunate to live "the endless summer." She adds: "If you can get up every day, surf perfect waves wherever you go—I mean, if you're enjoying that, winning a world title is just a bonus. For me, it was more what I went through to win it. My body was giving way on me in the end. To overcome that and win the title was great, but when I win any contest, I'm just as happy."

Mary Hartman, founder of Girl in the Curl surf shop and
Swell Times surfing school. Photo: Karin Moeller

The Surfing Way of Life

Getting paid to surf is the ultimate career goal of many surfers, but a reality for very few. Many men surfers, including former pros, have carved out careers for themselves in the surfing industry—as surfboard shapers, surf shop owners, surf photographers, surf apparel designers, journalists, artists, engineers, marketers and entrepreneurs. Nearly all surf apparel and surfboard companies, and the satellite businesses related to them, began as garage operations, nurtured by surfers committed to improving the sport with their product and making a living doing it.

Similar business opportunities for women surfers have been more elusive. However, several women have fashioned solid niches for themselves. In 1977, while still competing on the pro circuit, Margo Oberg started her Surfing School on Kauai, still in operation today. Other seventies pros Nancy Emerson and Betty Depolito also continued their involvement in the sport. Emerson runs a surfing school headquartered on Maui, offering one-hour lessons or one-week surf clinics in Maui, Australia and Fiji. As Banzai Betty, Depolito enjoys a career as writer, surf video producer and columnist.

Carving Careers

In 1995, Ilona Wood started a mini-revolution when she opened Water Girl, the first women-only surf shop in Encinitas, California. The shop provided a place where women could try on bathing suits, wetsuits and other apparel in the comfort of a woman-friendly atmosphere. They could ask questions that they were too intimidated to ask at regular surf shops. The store created a sensation and other women have followed her lead.

Mary Hartman, owner of Swell Times Surf School since 1985, was among the first to visit the newly-opened Water Girl. "I was so excited that I decided to open my own store in Orange County and call it Girl in the Curl," she says. On a subsequent boat trip to Costa Rica, Hartman spent her non-surfing time designing the store layout and logo. "I had been seeing more girls coming in for lessons. I felt there was a need for a shop where girls could go to talk surf and do positive things together like beach cleanups." Opening the business was a challenge, says Hartman. "I couldn't get a bank loan. I had to borrow money on two credit cards and from my brother and mother. But, on the day I opened, I sold a surfboard and business has been great since."

Hartman feels the biggest issue that aspiring women surfers need to work on is fear of the ocean. "Some aren't very good swimmers, so they're not confident in the water.

Jeannie Chesser's "Jaws" design.
Photo: Jeannie Chesser

In lessons, I start them out on soft boards and stay close to shore where they can almost touch bottom. I explain that sharks don't really like being in the lineup or where waves break. We don't see that many along this coastline anyway."

The hardest part of running her business, says Hartman, is finding the time required to do everything. "People say you're married to a retail store. No way—this store is *my baby*," she adds, laughing. "I created this beautiful life, now I'm nurturing it and helping it grow."

At the same time Hartman was nurturing Girl in the Curl, the seed of a similar idea was germinating among three surfing girlfriends in Santa Cruz, California. In November 1997, Paradise Surf Shop was born. Owners Sally Smith, Kristina Marquez and Alayna Schiebel each brought something unique to the business. Smith, thirty-eight, had been a legal assistant for nineteen years. Marquez, thirty-five, had twelve years experience as a surf shop manager on the North Shore and an illustrious surfing family background as daughter of San Onofre regular Gretchen Van Dyke and niece of big wave veteran Fred Van Dyke. Schiebel, twenty-six, was a competitive surfer. "From the beginning, our mission has been to provide a surf shop where women feel

comfortable," says Smith. "Whether they are novices or pros, or too intimidated to talk to a guy about surfing or embarrassed to try on a wetsuit." Santa Cruz surfing women enjoy Paradise Surf contests and clinics, as well as programs on breast cancer and skin cancer awareness, and local environmental issues. Novices seeking lessons are referred to It's A Girl Thing Surf School, run by former pro Anne Bayly. Smith says, "People get excited about what we're doing."

S.H.E. Surfs is stirring up excitement in Satellite Beach, Florida. Founder Lisa Wolfe opened the store in 1998 after spending several years in retail and in various jobs in the surf industry, including modeling and repping. Wolfe was an Army brat who moved to Florida in 1980 with her family when she was nine. Family time was spent together on weekends at the beach during the summer. "With three fabulous brothers, I thought I was one of them and had to try everything they did, including surfing. My first attempts at surfing were on a severely used and dinged-up Natural Arts board that I shared with my brothers."

Top: Paradise Surf founders Kristina Marquez, Alayna Schiebel and Sally Smith. Photo: Courtesy Paradise Surf

Bottom: Frieda Zamba teaches clinics for S.H.E. Surfs. Photo: Lisa Wolfe

Wolfe had no aspirations of being a pro. "I always wanted a shop of my own. I remember sitting in my favorite climbing tree in the backyard, drawing and designing apartments and shops that I would live in and work in with all my wonderful friends. That began in the third grade. After helping friends in their various stores, I knew the theme [for her business] would be surf."

The most successful part of S.H.E. Surfs is the series of instructional clinics held once a month from April through September, conducted by world champion Frieda Zamba. The first clinic was held in May 1999; a hundred girls showed up. "We had perfect surf-

ing conditions and perfect weather. The girls had a blast, the parents enjoyed watching and the sponsors had their exact market as a captive audience for an entire day. It was a huge success," says Wolfe. "Now the guys in town can't wait until we do clinics, because we always seem to get great surf."

Zamba was one of her biggest promoters, says Wolfe. "Frieda is humble, gracious and the kids love her. She also rips!" S.H.E. Surfs sponsors Falina Spires, another promising product of Florida's surf culture. Spires often assists Zamba during clinics. They are a big draw, says Wolfe. "The clinics are always full, with a waiting list."

When asked what S.H.E. stands for, Wolfe explains that it is just a "marketing thing," and adds, "I have sort of an ongoing contest for the kids in town, to come up with what it means. The best one so far is from a thirteen-year-old boy: Surfing Has Evolved."

Women's surf camps also are evolving. One of the most interesting is Las Olas, founded by Bev Sanders. In 1997, needing a break from their snowboarding business (Avalanche Snowboards, which they founded in 1981), Sanders and her husband decided to vacation in Hawaii. As her husband picked up a book and settled into a plush chair on the lanai, Sanders decided to seek a different sort of relaxation. "I saw an ad for Nancy Emerson's School of Surfing. It showed a dog riding a surfboard and the caption, 'If a dog can surf, so can you.' I took a lesson." At forty-four, Sanders found herself hooked on a new sport.

In November that year, Sanders, Izzy Tihanyi of Surf Diva surf school and a few friends journeyed to a surf spot in Mexico about forty minutes above Puerto Vallarta. "The whole time, Izzy and I talked about what we could do to get more women involved in surfing," says Sanders. "It is such an empowering sport." The result of their

S.H.E. Surfs clinics are a big draw in
Florida. Photo: Lisa Wolfe

125

ruminations is Las Olas ("the waves"), a surf camp for women (near the same spot above Puerto Vallarta) that includes surfing instruction and gear, plus daily yoga lessons and massage. Surf Diva is contracted to provide instruction. "Izzy and I didn't want to be partners. We're both independent," says Sanders. "It's a good arrangement."

Las Olas appeals to the sensibilities of women. "Simple elegance, but natural," Sanders explains. "The villas are built among the trees. You know you're on vacation. We get women twenty-three to fifty-five, from all walks of life: scientists, waitresses, doctors, veterinarians and moms. We dine family style every night and mix it up, to prevent cliques."

Starting a business in the surf industry has been an eye opener, says Sanders. "I have never come across such camaraderie. In snowboarding, which is very male dominated, there is so much competition and posturing. The women I've encountered in surfing are willing to help promote each other. We realize everyone wins. Women are great networkers—in business as well as in the water."

Marilyn Edwards and Elizabeth Glazner used all their networking powers to start *Wahine* magazine in 1995. They first met in August 1993. Edwards, a speech pathologist, had recently begun surfing again, after many years out of the water. Glazner, a journalist, had always wanted to learn to surf. They became friends and started surfing together.

During their first few surfing adventures around Seal Beach, Bolsa Chica and San Onofre, they talked about the lack of female representation in the surf industry—especially in the magazines, which tended to relegate women to the status of faceless tarts in thong bikinis. One day Edwards remarked, "I've always wanted to start a women's surfing magazine," and Glazner said, "Let's do it!"

Glazner quit her job as lifestyle editor for a daily newspaper and moved to Long Beach to set up the first *Wahine* homestead in the small therapy office Edwards used for her private practice. Instead of a business plan, they wrote a media kit, devoid of photo images of women surfers. They mailed the kit to all the companies whose business cards they had collected at a surfing trade show, and sold about eight ads. They took out a line of credit from the bank, and hocked Edward's vintage Porsche in order to print the first issue.

Wahine threw a launch party during the U.S. Open of Surfing in

Top: Bev Sanders, founder of Las Olas.
Photo: Patty Segovia—Silver Photo Agency

Bottom: Las Olas makes girls out of women. Photo: Patty Segovia

July 1995, at the International Surfing Museum in Huntington Beach. Hundreds of people came to celebrate the first women's surf magazine and to hear the all-girl neo-surf instrumental band the Neptunas. Back at the office, Glazner continued to freelance for other publications to pay her bills, while building the editorial infrastructure of *Wahine*. Edwards studied balance sheets and entered subscriptions long into the night, while still directing the speech and hearing clinic at Long Beach City College. From the beginning, *Wahine* was a hit.

Jeannie Chesser is a hit announcer in Hawaii. When a women's contest organizer needs an announcer or a judge, the person likely to get the call is Jeannie Chesser. When someone needs a custom paint job on a new surfboard, Chesser is the artist. Surfers headed to Diamond Head, Ala Moana or Waikiki first call Chesser's hotline for a current surf report. There was never any doubt that Chesser would make a living from surfing; her life revolves around it. "Everything I've done has come to me," she says. "I've never pursued anything."

Originally from Florida, Chesser learned to surf in 1964 at Daytona Beach when she was fourteen. "As a kid, I was always in the water in some way, either on a boat or a surfboard." After her husband died in 1971, Chesser took their two-year-old son, Todd, and moved to Hawaii to start anew. Todd had already taken to the water as a baby. With perfect, challenging surf at his doorstep, he developed into a talented and respected big wave surfer. Chesser became "surf mom" to all his surfing friends. Tragically, in 1998 Todd lost his life while surfing the waves he loved. "The ocean gives life and takes life," says Chesser. "It's an enigma. It's still a source of meditation, but also a source of fear."

Chesser remains a surf mom to Todd's friends, who leave their cars in her yard while out surfing and regularly check in on her and take her to dinner and parties. Through her business, Surfing Arts, Chesser has painted surfboards for twenty-five years. She regularly paints for Hawaiian Island Creations' surfboard factory and also does custom jobs. She judges and announces when needed, and surfs nearly every day. From her house on the back slopes of Diamond Head, Chesser can hear the ocean but can't see it. She doesn't need to. She feels its rhythms. The surf surges in her blood. "Todd's death inspired me to keep surfing," she says. "I know that's what he'd want me to do. He loved the ocean as much as I do. I'll never leave it."

Top: Newly-stoked surfers at S.H.E. Surfs clinic. Photo: Lisa Wolfe

Bottom: Jeannie Chesser displays some of her "Surfing Art." Photo: Bernie Baker

127

Surf Diva Izzy

By Karin Moeller

Isabelle "Izzy" Tihanyi founded the first all-women's surf school in La Jolla, California, in 1996. Called Surf Diva, the name was Tihanyi's inspiration. "A diva is a woman who knows herself and can assert herself," she says. "She knows what she wants and knows how to get it. FloJo was a diva, Queen Latifah is a diva, Madonna is a diva and Rell Sun was a diva. It used to be that you had to pick between being a jock and a girl, but now you can be both. A surf diva is as comfortable in her board shorts as she is in her Versace dress."

Originally run from Tihanyi's house, Surf Diva now operates from a storefront office space. Tihanyi and her staff of expert women surfers teach up to one hundred students a week through weekend clinics, five-day clinics, teen camps and private lessons. Surf Diva also provides instruction for Las Olas women's surf camp in Mexico.

A San Diego native, Tihanyi started surfing at age six and was immediately hooked. "Jericho Poppler was one of my idols as a kid," says Tihanyi. "She had her name spray-painted in red on the back of her board and I thought, 'Wow, that's cool!'" But like Poppler and other female surfers of her generation, Tihanyi was generally alone among men in the water. "Growing up, I didn't have any other women in the water, and it was lonely out there," she says. "There was a need to teach women in a fun, caring, nurturing environment. Guys can get lessons anywhere. I wanted to take care of the girls."

That's not to say that Surf Diva doesn't have male clients—many of Tihanyi's group lessons include male students—but women dominate the attendance. They all benefit. "Sometimes, customers come in stressed out, and by the time we're through with them they're different people." She adds, "Surfing almost becomes an obsession. Put it this way: If there's a really good swell and Nordstrom's is having their big sale, I know what *I'm* doing."

The number of women seeking out Surf Diva to get a surf-inspired attitude adjustment has increased steadily. 1999 was an exceptional year for exposure: The company was written up in the *Wall Street Journal, Cosmopolitan, Shape, Elle, Condé Naste Women's Sports & Fitness, Jump, Teen, Business Start-Ups* and *Teen People*. Tihanyi and crew have been on *Extra, Good Morning America*, The Learning Channel, The Travel Channel and international TV programs in Brazil and Germany. The client list keeps growing.

Surf Diva Izzy Tihanyi.
Photo: Tomas Gibson

"Owning a business has forced me to learn about so many things—accounting, taxes, licensing, permits, insurance, payroll, hiring, budgets, interviewing. I've really had to grow up," says Tihanyi. "But now I want to start ten more businesses. I dream of running a surf company someday—clothing, boards, instruction—the whole lifestyle as a package so I can travel to great surf spots. I hope to be involved with Surf Diva for the rest of my life."

1998 Las Olas attendees and instructors. Izzy is standing, third from left. Photo: Patty Segovia Silver Photo Agency

Kauai's Koral McCarthy walks the nose.
Photo: Jim Russi

Millennium Stars

What do Megan Abubo, Melanie Bartels, Holly Beck, Jenny Boggis, Tanya Booth, Heather Clark, Amee Donoghoe, Keala Kennelly, Koral McCarthy, Kassia Meador, Sofia Mulanovich, Jodie Nelson, Kristin Quizon, Sena Seramur, Daize Shayne, Falina Spires and Tita Tavares have in common? **21st Century Wahines**

They are all surfers poised to master women's surfing in the new millennium. These young women, and scores of other young women are breaking open new territory in the water. Some will become pros and world champions. Others will soul surf to the end of their days. A few may turn their surfing passion into a business.

Several will set out to surf the world, as Ashley Carney and Chris Zeitler did beginning in December 1999. Calling themselves the Sol Sirens, the women documented their odyssey on camera and plan to release a commercial video upon their return. Their goal, says Carney, is to "reach out to girls who aren't pros, who surf because they love it. Encourage them to get out and travel and have fun."

Amateur programs, such as the National Scholastic Surfing Association (NSSA), founded in 1978, encourage young women to have fun in a community of like-minded competitors. The NSSA has blossomed from a small, local surfing association into the highest profile amateur competitive surfing association in the U.S., with over two thousand active members. Although there is a special emphasis on student surfers, the NSSA is open to anyone who wants to surf competitively as an amateur. For many successful ASP surfers—including Hawaii's Megan Abubo—the NSSA has been a springboard to the pros.

A visible NSSA champion and rising star is nineteen-year-old Holly Beck from Palos Verdes, California.

Peru's surfing sensation, Sofia Mulanovich. Photo: Jeff Hornbaker

The oldest of five sisters, Beck started surfing in 1995. She dominated the women's division of the NSSA while in high school. Now, as a student at UC-San Diego, Beck is balancing a burgeoning modeling career with surfing, while also working towards a degree in management science. "Surfing has had a huge impact on my life," says Beck, who can walk from her dorm down the cliff to Black's Beach and surf for a couple of hours before calculus class. "I get my homework done so I can go surfing. I keep my grades up so I can go surfing. It's a motivation for everything I do."

Kristin Quizon arrived at the Roxy Pro in Sunset Beach in December 1999 as a wild card entry to the contest. She was fifteen, the youngest competitor. It was her first pro event. She had prepared for this moment since her father taught her to surf at Ewa Beach as a child. "I admire my dad so much," she shared after her heat. "He's not only a good surfer but a good father. He makes many sacrifices for me and my family."

Quizon decided to turn pro in 1998. "I started doing amateur contests and started placing and getting sponsors, such as Roxy. I figured I had potential. I want to be a successful person and do what I am supposed to do as a surfer. Go full on and help others, like Rell Sunn. Have a good attitude towards people and find myself." Quizon got a glimpse of herself as a pro surfer when, to her delight, she advanced to the quarter finals at Sunset Beach.

Fifteen-year-old San Clemente surfer Tanya Booth entered the junior women's amateur division in

Top: Kristin Quizon of Hawaii heads for her first pro heat at Sunset Beach. Photo: Andrea Gabbard

Bottom: Hawaii's Melanie Bartels. Photo: Jim Russi

Hawaii's world title contender, Megan Abubo.
Photo: Jim Russi

133

2000. She started surfing at age nine and competing in 1997. She consistently places in the top three, if not number one. Her hero is Abubo. "She is always challenging herself," says Booth. "She's fun, really nice, and she rips." Booth currently rides a longboard but is going to expand her repertoire to include a shortboard. She travels up and down the coast with her father, brother and sister, surfing from Malibu to San Diego. Booth aspires to be a model and, she says, "maybe a pro surfer," although, she adds, "I don't know if I could make a living off it. Right now, I surf for fun."

Keala Kennelly from Kauai has her sights set on the world championship. After five years in qualifying series contests, she entered her first full year on the WCT tour in 2000. Tall, tough and radical, twenty-two-year-old Kennelly has been called "the bad child" of surfing for her outspokenness. In truth, she is a sensitive and

Keala Kennelly wants to "own" a world
title. Photo: Tom Servais

caring individual . . . on land. In the water, she becomes a barreling, airborne, cut-back machine with one goal in mind: to win the world championship. "I want to *own* a world title," she says. "And I'm willing to work for it. When I first started out, I didn't want to surf like anyone else. I was a little hotheaded smartass who thought she could beat anybody." Many pros will be watching over their shoulders for Kennelly to advance to the top ranks.

Kennelly also is outspoken about the need for women's surfing to be depicted realistically. "People want to see honesty," she says. "They want to see who the pro surfers really are. They don't want companies to dress up a girl who can't really surf and do this whole image thing that is really a lie. I'd like to see our organization develop a program where every girl on tour has a sponsor. There would be no envy or jealousy among the girls about who's getting what. That would be a beautiful thing."

A lovely sight on a balmy October day is San Onofre's Roxy Wahine Classic, an amateur contest produced by surfer/entrepreneur Allan Seymour. The contest attracts over two hundred female surfers, age seven to seventy. Often, a few "legends" show up to compete in the Masters division, but the biggest turnout is among girls eight to nineteen. Young surfing talent also can be found at other amateur events, including Rell Sunn's Menehune Contest in Hawaii each November and the East Coast Wahines contest in August in Wrightsville Beach, North Carolina, which attracts girls from as far away as New Jersey and Florida.

Top left: Lauren Cody wants to be a pro. Photo: Karin Moeller

Bottom left: Colleen Mehlburg plans to be a marine biologist. Photo: Karin Moeller

Top right: Jessica Silver has been surfing since age four. Photo: Karin Moeller

Bottom right: Katie Nelson scores an autograph from the real Gidget, Kathy Kohner. Photo: Karin Moeller

Amateur events are the sport's breeding ground, and they also teach young women about strength, showmanship and sisterhood. Nine-year-old Lauren Cody, a lively towhead of nine, competed in the Teenie Weenie Wahine division at San Onofre in 1999, after having learned to surf that summer. "It was kind of scary, but really fun. That's why I do it," she gushed after her heat. "I want to be a pro. I like to watch Holly Beck."

Her co-competitor, redheaded Jessie Silver, age ten, had six years more experience. She placed fourth in her heat. Silver's father is a surfer. He said, "She doesn't want to play soccer. She doesn't want to play softball. She just wants to surf. I love it because the rest of the dads are soccer dads, stuck all day at the soccer field, while I get to go to the beach."

Colleen Mehlburg started surfing at age nine. Before she was strong enough to paddle, her father would push her board into waves. At twelve, and very composed, she won her heat at the 1999 San Onofre meet. Mehlburg had this to say about surfing: "I like that it's free, you can do what you want. There are no rules, no limitations; it's all about yourself and pushing yourself. You have your own style, and you can do what you want, be who you are. I think surfing should be for the fun of it, not just to show people what you can do." This, after wowing the crowd on the beach with a display of walking the nose, falling and recovering, then doing a dying cockroach followed by a headstand.

Mehlburg adds that she does not intend to make a living from surfing. "I'd like to be a marine biologist," she says, "so that I can always be at the ocean and help save the environment."

At these amateur events, the kids really clean up with free stickers, posters and, for prizes, everything from koa-wood bowls and T-shirts to leashes and surfboards. Katie Nelson, fourteen, has been surfing for six years and lives in Laguna Beach, California. She's surfed in Hawaii with her family. Her surfing hero is longboarder Daize Shayne. "In Ventura at a contest last year, I was there alone, and she helped me, talked to me so that I didn't feel like

Sena Seramur, Hawaiian amateur
champ. Photo: Jim Russi

Longboard champion Daize
Shayne and fans. Photo: Jim Russi

a loner. I felt like I belonged, thanks to Daize."

Nelson plans to make her living as a movie director and save surfing for fun. She loves meeting new people through surfing and, she adds, "I also like all the stuff you get from it." New surfboards, leashes and koa bowls? "No," she says, "like emotionally and spiritually—you get a lot of goodness in your heart from surfing."

Floridian Falina Spires was coached by
Frieda Zamba. Photo: Jim Russi

Surfing Legacies

By Karin Moeller

Among surfing families, water skills are passed from generation to generation like heirlooms. In Hawaii, former world champion Anona Napoleon and her husband, Nappy, taught all five of their children to surf. Today, they are teaching their grandchildren. Says Anona, "When you're in the ocean, there's a sense of being one with all of creation." These feelings are also transmitted to grandchildren. "It's so satisfying to hear the kids say, 'I caught that wave all by myself, you didn't have to push me.' I see in them a part of myself. I see the time when I told my father, over fifty years ago, 'Hey, Dad, I did it by myself, you didn't have to push me.'"

Since the thirties, parents have been pushing their kids into the surf at one of Southern California's most famous family beaches, San Onofre. That's where, back in the summer of 1954, Liz and Jim Irwin met and forged a beach lifestyle that endures to this day.

Their marriage produced two daughters, Wendy and Heidi, as well as forty-four years—and counting—worth of beach and surf experiences. Jim, known as the Golden Voice of San Onofre, has announced surf contests for nearly half a century, starting in the sixties with the World Championships in Huntington Beach. Liz, once a synchronized swimmer and Polynesian dancer, surfed for close to forty years and captured her first first-place surf ranking at age fifty.

On weekends, the Irwin family would drive two hours from Los Angeles to San Onofre. This was long before the freeway system was developed, when Highway 101 meandered through the now-overwhelmed orange groves of Orange County. "It was particularly charming when we'd see another car 'on surfari,'" says Liz. "We'd pull over, stop and chat about our trips and experiences. There was a time when you'd know every other surfer out in the water—it was such a great community." One of the most notable Irwin family story lines came in the form of surfing success for daughter Wendy, who answered the ocean's call in the womb three weeks early and sent her mother into labor at San Onofre.

By age seven, the prenatal link manifested itself and Wendy began surfing, wearing only a life preserver and trunks. She had already taken to waterskiing, basketball, skiing, skateboarding and baseball, so surfing came easily. A year later, the surf ingénue had her first taste of success, sweeping the "Eight and Under" category as the only girl. "I was doing headstands, spinners, ballet poses," remembers Wendy Irwin Gilley. "I kicked butt!"

Wendy Gilley, age 7.
Photo: Irwin collection

Little girls kicking butt in the surf, especially in the late sixties, was indeed a rarity. "It was always a novelty for the boys to see a girl out there," says Gilley. "But whenever I went out, I gave a hundred percent, so I've always been given respect. The guys were always encouraging."

It was the beginning of a long and successful romance with surfing. Her ten-year professional career, from 1975 to 1985, included the 1983 highlight of placing second behind Oberg in the World Cup at Sunset Beach. Now married, Gilley is passing the surfing legacy to her two sons. She shares her gift for teaching as program director for Mary Setterholm's Surf Academy in Manhattan Beach. Gilley calls surfing a way of life. "You're always thinking about your next trip or your last session. It keeps you close to nature and close to God. It teaches you how to be humble. As Rell Sunn demonstrated in her life, it's all about Aloha—give of yourself and it will come back to you."

The Aloha spirit is shared by longtime friends and surfing buddies Michelle Goossen and Jere Becker, who regularly meet at San Onofre to surf. Now in their forties, both grew up surfing in Southern California. Becker started surfing Poche and Doheny, then concentrated on Huntington Beach until 1994, when she was diagnosed with breast cancer. "I had a choice of driving to Hollywood or to Carlsbad for radiation," she says. "A friend had a condo in San Clemente and invited me to

Bottom: Liz, Jim, Heidi and Wendy Irwin Photo: Irwin collection

Top: Liz Irwin taught Sunday School classes on the bluffs overlooking San Onofre. Photo: Irwin collection

see that no matter how old you get, no matter what your body habitus is, or how many babies you have, you can still get back out there and surf for the rest of your life."

Becker adds, "There aren't a lot of sports where you can continue to do that. Your knees give out for running and tennis. I've given up volleyball and snow skiing. The only thing that is left is surfing."

"I'm never going to stop surfing," says Goosen. "When I'm eighty, they can put me on a softboard and push me out into the whitewater and I'll ride it on my stomach."

She will ride with those who have gone before her—the ancient Polynesians, the Ali'i, the *kupua,* family and friends. Gilley says that her longtime friend, Rell Sunn, often visits her in the water. "I'm not the only one who feels her presence since she passed on," says Gilley. "When I do a soul arch or a cheater five, I feel Rell surfing through me. It's a gift of happiness."

The joy of riding a wave never leaves a surfer.

stay there, so I started surfing, too, at San Onofre. Now I know all the old-timers."

San Onofre is not a body-conscious beach, says Goossen, who has surfed there since a child. "The age range is eighty down. You don't see thongs here. If you've got a little belly or have some cottage cheese going on, it doesn't matter. The guys like to see you out here. When I went to medical school, I'd come down to San-O and study. The kids on the beach would help quiz me. We'd set a timer and when the dinger went off, they'd say, 'Okay, time for a surf break!'"

About four years ago, Goossen's daughters took up the sport. Candace, fifteen, and Shelly, eighteen, now surf on the team at San Clemente High School. "They get up early every morning and show up at the pier to surf before school," says Goossen. "Jere and I aren't competitive surfers. We do it because we want the young girls to

Surf buddies Michelle Goosen and Jere Becker. Photo: Andrea Gabbard

GLOSSARY

AERIALS: maneuvers that result in surfer and surfboard launching off a wave into the air.

BAIL OUT: jumping off a surfboard before wiping out.

BARREL: see "Tube" and "Shooting the Tube."

BEACH BREAK: a wave that breaks close to the shore of the beach (also SHORE BREAK).

BLOW HOLE: a place where currents and bottom configuration cause a whirlpool that sucks in water and spews it out.

BLOWN OUT: when high winds cause the surf to be choppy and unrideable.

BLUEBIRD: a beautiful wave approaching outside.

BOIL: a churning, bubbly spot in the water created by current and configuration of the bottom.

BOTTOM TURN: a turn at the bottom of the wall of the front of the wave.

BOWL: the section of wave between the tube and shoulder; a shallow spot in the path of the wave that causes it to break faster or harder.

BREAK: a term for waves in a particular area.

CHANNEL: a deep spot where waves don't normally break.

CHAT ROOM: a group of surfers sitting together, talking, in the water.

CHEATER FIVE: placing the toes of one foot on or over the nose of the board while riding (also HANGING FIVE).

CLIMB AND DROP: a maneuver where the rider goes to the crest of the wave then comes back down the face towards the bottom.

CLOSE OUT: when a wave breaks simultaneously across its entire length; when waves break across a bay or normally safe channel.

COMBER: a wave.

CREST: the highest point of a wave before it breaks.

CURL: the breaking part of a wave.

CUSTOM BOARD: A surfboard built with the rider's height, weight and surfing style in mind.

CUT-BACK: to turn back, while riding, toward the curl or breaking part of a wave.

DECK: the top of a surfboard.

DING: a hole or scratch on a surfboard.

DROP: the initial downward slide on the wave after taking off.

DROP IN: taking off on a wave on which there is already a rider; bad manners.

FACE: the unbroken front of a wave between the crest and the trough where the surfer rides.

FIN: the appendage on the tail of the surfboard that acts like a rudder to facilitate turning (also SKEG).

FLAT: no waves, no surf.

FLOATER: a maneuver where the surfer rides over the falling curtain of a wave.

GIRL BOARDS: Joe Quigg's 1950 balsawood surfboards, featuring a revolutionary rocker design and shorter length, for the women who were surfing Malibu at the time.

GLASS-OFF: when the wind dies (early morning, late afternoon), causing the water to become very smooth.

GLASSY: when there is no wind and the surface of the water is extremely smooth, giving it a glassy reflection.

GOOFY-FOOT: a surfer who rides with right foot forward.

GRABBING THE RAIL: holding on to the outside rail of the surfboard, to avoid being knocked off or to perfect your trim on the wave.

GROMMET: a young surfer (also GROM, GREMMIE).

GROVEL BOARD: a shortboard used in small surf of one-to-two feet.

GUN: a long board used for riding big waves.

HANGING FIVE: placing the toes of one foot over the nose of the board while riding (also CHEATER FIVE).

HANG TEN: placing the toes of both feet over the nose of the board while riding.

HAOLE: Hawaiian for Caucasian.

HEAD DIP: while riding, the surfer crouches as the lip of the wave wets her head.

HOME BREAK: where a surfer learned to surf or consistently surfs.

HOT DOGGING: to perform or show a great surfing ability, denoted by fancy turns, walking the nose and other radical moves.

IMPACT ZONE: the area inside where waves have broken, creating whitewater; in big surf, the most dangerous place to get caught (also THE ZONE).

INSIDE: shoreward of the normal breaking point of the waves; getting "caught inside" is to be in the impact zone.

LEASH: the cord attached from the surfboard to the surfer's ankle.

LEFT: used to describe waves that break from right to left, from the rider's point of view.

LINEUP: the take-off area; a fixed position where the waves consistently break, commonly configured by landmarks, rocks or boils in the water.

LIP: the fringing crest of the wave starting to break or curl.

MALIBU BOARD: balsawood surfboards designed in the late forties and ridden predominantly in Malibu; also called chips or potato chips.

MENEHUNE: Hawaiian word for young boy or girl.

MUSHY: describes a slow, sloppy wave that has little power.

NATURAL FOOT: a surfer who rides with left foot forward.

OFFSHORE: when the wind blows from the land out to sea (produces the best waves).

ONSHORE: when the wind blows from behind the waves (flattens or chops up the waves).

OUTSIDE: the area seaward or behind the breaking surf; also used to announce an approaching set of waves—i.e., "Outside!"

PEAK: the part of the wave that breaks first.

PEARL: when the nose of the surfboard goes underneath the surface of the water on takeoff, usually resulting in a wipe out.

POINT BREAK: a wave that breaks from left to right or vice versa from a point that extends from the coastline.

PRO/AM: an event that includes both professional and amateur participants.

PULL-OUT: ending the ride by steering the board over or through the back of the wave.

QUIVER: a surfer's collection of boards, each designed for different wave conditions.

RAILS: the rounded edges of a surfboard.

REEF BREAK: a wave that breaks over a submerged line or ridge of rock or coral.

REENTRY: a maneuver where the surfer cuts into the lip vertically, then turns the board nose down and reenters the wave.

RIGHT: used to describe waves that break from left to right, from the rider's point of view.

RIP or RIPPING: an aggressive or radical maneuver on a wave; an aggressive, radical style of surfing.

ROCKER: the amount of curve from tip to tail of a surfboard; one end can have more curve than the other to achieve different effects.

SET: a group of waves that breaks in a pattern, one after another.

SHAPER: the person who makes a surfboard by "shaping" the foam (or, in the past, the balsa- or redwood).

SHOOT THE TUBE (also SHOOT THE CURL, GET BARRELED, GET TUBED, TUBE RIDE): crouching through the most hollow portion of a wave and making it through.

SHORE BREAK: waves that break very close to shore (also BEACH BREAK).

SHOULDER: the end section of a wave that has not yet broken.

SKEG: the fin or rudder of a surfboard.

SLOT: the perfect spot in the wave.

SOUL ARCH: while riding, the surfer leans back, feet together, with her back in an arch, arms overhead.

SPINNER: turning around on a surfboard until you face the same direction in which you started; also called a 360.

STICK: a surfboard.

STOKED: a positive exclamation; i.e., "I'm stoked! I just got barreled!"

SURF'S UP: used to describe the condition when the waves are especially good for surfing.

SWELL: either one unbroken wave or all of the waves coming from a particular storm.

TAKEOFF or TAKING OFF: the point at which the surfer catches the wave and stands up.

TAKE GAS: see WIPE OUT.

TAIL: the rear of the board to which the fin or skeg is attached.

TANDEM: two people riding a surfboard.

TOES-ON-THE-NOSE: see HANGING FIVE or HANG TEN.

TOP TURN: similar to reentry, with a less vertical approach; used to gain speed on a wave.

TOW-IN SURFING: using a personal watercraft to pull a surfer into a large wave.

TRIM or TRIMMING: steering the board parallel with the line of the wave to generate the most possible speed on your surfboard.

TUBE or BARREL: the hollow formed by a curling wave (see SHOOT THE TUBE).

WAHINE: "girl" in Hawaiian; also, a female surfer.

WALK: walking forward or backward on a surfboard.

WALK THE NOSE: cross-stepping towards the nose of the board.

WALL: the face of a wave before it has broken.

WATERMAN/WATERWOMAN: a person who is proficient at many self-propelled watersports, such as surfing, outrigger canoe paddling, free diving.

WAX: paraffin wax rubbed on the deck of a surfboard to help your feet grip it.

WHITEWATER or WHITEWASH: the foamy part of the wave after it breaks; also called soup, foam or froth.

WIPE OUT: falling off your surfboard while riding a wave; also known as taking gas.

THE ZONE: see IMPACT ZONE.

RESOURCES

ORGANIZATIONS

Association of Surfing
Professionals (ASP)
Coolangatta, QLD Australia
61-7-5599-1550
www.aspworldtour.com

ASP/North America
Laguna Beach, CA
949/366-4584

Association of Women
Surfers (AWS)
P.O. Box 2031
Santa Cruz, CA 95063
831/469-9991

Eastern Surfing Association
(ESA)
P.O. Box 582
Ocean City, MD 21843
1-800-WE SHRED

International Surfing
Association (ISA)
World Headquarters
470 Nautilus #300
La Jolla, CA 92037
PH 619/551-5292
FX 619/551-5290

National Scholastic Surfing
Association (NSSA)
National Office
P.O. Box 495
Huntington Beach, CA 92648
PH 714/536-0445
FX 714/960-4380
jaragon@nssa.org
www.nssa.org

Surfrider Foundation USA
122 S. El Camino Real #67
San Clemente, CA 92672
PH 949/492-8170
FX 949/492-8142
Info@surfrider.org
www.surfrider.org

United States Surfing
Federation (USSF)
(Formerly U.S.Surfing
Association)
7104 Island Village Drive
Long Beach, CA 90803
562/596-7785

Waterwomen, Inc.
P.O. Box 293
Cardiff by the Sea, CA 92007
760/603-0029
www.wahinemagazine.com

WOMEN'S SURF SHOPS, CLINICS, SCHOOLS

WEST COAST

Girl in the Curl
34116 Pacific Coast Hwy.
Dana Point, CA 92677
949/661-4475
www.girlinthecurl.com

It's A Girl Thing Surf School
P.O. Box 1255
Capitola, CA 95010
831/462-5873
www.girlthingsurfschool.com

On Edge Girl's Board Shop
22311 Brookhurst St.
Huntington Beach, CA 92646
714/945-WAVE

Paradise Surf Shop
3961 Portola Dr.
Santa Cruz, CA 95062
831/462-3880
www.paradisesurf.com

Pink Lava Women's Surf
Shop
6780 La Jolla Blvd.
La Jolla, CA 92037
858/456-1165
www.pinklava.com

Rip Girl
321 Pier Ave.
Hermosa Beach, CA 90254
310/372-8756

Salty Sister
2796 Carlsbad Blvd.
Carlsbad, CA 92008
760/434-1122
www.saltysister.com

Sea Jane Surf
600 N. Catalina
Redondo Beach, CA 90277
310/937-2856
www.divensurf.com

Surf Academy
1246 8th St.
Manhattan Beach, CA 90266
310/372-2790
www.surfacademy.org

Surf City Surf Lessons
P.O. Box 3013
Huntington Beach, CA
92605-3013
714/898-2088

Surf Diva Surf School
2160-A Ave. de la Playa
La Jolla, CA 92037
858/454-8273
www.surfdiva.com

Surf Like A Girl
321 Pier Ave.
Hermosa Beach, CA 90254
310/372-8756
www.surf-like-a-girl.com

Swell Times Surf School
Dana Point, CA
(see Girl in the Curl listing)

Water Girl
642 S. Coast Hwy 101
Encinitas, CA 92024
760/436-2408
www.watergirl.com

EAST COAST

Chicks on Sticks (Surf Club)
P.O. Box 621
Narragansett, RI 02882
401/789-1336
link through
www.warmwinds.com
kira@uri.edu

East Coast Wahines
Championships
Anne Beasley, Event
Coordinator
949/361-5144
www.eastcoastwahines.com

Hot Tamales
4510 B Hoggard Dr.
Wilmington, NC 28403
910/233-3861

Inner Rhythm Surfer Girl
2001 14th Ave.
Vero Beach, FL 92060
561/778-9038

Ocean Divas (Surf Club)
158 Fletcher Ave.
Manasquan, NJ 08736
732/223-7750
madlog@bytheshore.com

Outer Banks Wahines (Surf
Club)
P.O. Box 2796
Kill Devil Hills, NC 27948

S.H.E. Surfs (Retail Shop &
Surf Clinic)
PO Box 372277
Satellite Beach, FL 32937
321/779-0115
www.she-surfs.com

Sisters of the Sea (Surf Club)
Eva Duran
436 Lora St.
Neptune Beach, FL 32266
904/241-4761
www.radicalside.com
ocean77537@aol.com

HAWAII

Honolua Wahine
2435 Kaanapali Pkwy., N3
Lahaina, HI 96761
808/661-3253
www.honoluasurf.com

Margo Oberg's Surfing
School
Nukumoi Surf Co.
Poipu Beach, Kauai
888/384-8810

Nancy Emerson School of
Surfing
P.O. Box 463
Lahaina, Maui, HI 96767
PH 808/874-1183
FX 808/874-2581
Ncesurf@maui.net
http://maui.net/~ncesurf/
ncesurf.html

AUSTRALIA

Women in Waves
Coolangatta Qld 4225
Australia
www.women-in-waves.com.au/

MEXICO

Las Olas Surf Adventures
for Women
991 Tyler St., Ste 101
Benicia, CA 94510
PH 707/746-6435
FX 707/745-2261
www.SurfLasOlas.com

ON-LINE RETAIL SHOPS

A Woman's Shape Surf Co.
(AWS)
www.awssurf.com

Chick Sticks
www.chicksticks.com

VIDEOS

Blue Crush
Billy Goat Productions
1905 Mackay Ln. Unit A
Redondo Beach, CA 90278
877/The-Goat; Outside US,
808/638-8137

Empress
Misty Productions
P.O. Box 1451
Carnelian Bay, CA 96140
530/546-9378
www.mistyproductions.com

Soaking Wet Girlz
By Banzai Betty
Banzai Productions
Box 572
Haleiwa, HI 96712
PH 808/638-8326
FX 808/638-5573

Surfer Girl
Donna Olson
P.O. Box 2226
Southampton, NY 11969
516/283-6432

Surfing for Life
David L. Brown Productions
415/468-7469
docmaker1@aol.com

SOURCE BOOKS

Doyle, Mike, with Sorenson,
Steve, *Morning Glass*, Three
Rivers: Manzanita Press,
1994

Finney, Ben and Houston,
James D., *Surfing, A History
of the Ancient Hawaiian
Sport*, San Francisco: Pome-
granate Books, 1996

Hemmings, Fred, *The Soul of
Surfing*, New York: Thunder's
Mouth Press, 1997

Stell, Marion K., *Pam
Burridge*, Australia: Angus &
Robertson, An imprint of

Harper Collins Publishers,
1992

Warshaw, Matt, *SurfRiders*,
New York: Collins Publishers, 1997

MAGAZINES

Carve
United Kingdom
www.orcasurf.co.uk

Chick
Burleigh Heads, QLD Australia
07-5576-1388
chick@morrisonmedia.com.au

Eastern Surf Magazine
Indialantic, FL 32903
www.easternsurf.com

ExtremeSports
(online only)
www.extremesports.com

Girls Surf Life
(online only)
www.GirlsSurfLife.com

Longboard
San Clemente, CA
949/366-8280

New Zealand Surfing
New Zealand
www.surfingnz.com

Surfer
San Juan Capistrano, CA
949/496-5922
www.surfermag.com

Surfer Girl
San Juan Capistrano, CA
949/496-5922

Surfer's Journal
San Clemente, CA
949/361-0331
www.surfersjournal.com

Surfing
San Clemente, CA

949/492-7873
www.surfingthemag.com

Surfing Girl
San Clemente, CA
949/492-7873
www.surfinggirl.com

Tracks
Australia
www.tracksmag.com

Wahine
Long Beach, CA
562/434-9444
www.wahinemagazine.com

Water Wahine
Online only
www.waterwahine.com

Waves
Australia
adam.blakey@emap.com.au

**Other foreign surf
magazines:**

Surfing World
Australia

Underground Surf
Australia

Revista Fluir
Brazil

Surf Session
France

Surfing World
Japan

Surfers Path
United Kingdom

Tres 60
Spain

Surf Portugal
Portugal

Surf Latino
Italy